The
Final Message

ALL life forms on Earth, including ourselves, were created by advanced human scientists from another part of our galaxy. They used sophisticated DNA genetic engineering techniques and now that we are approaching their level of achievement, they want to return here openly to meet major world leaders and the media . . .

These are the key points of momentous claims made in *The Final Message* by Claude Raël. He says the scientists, who call themselves 'the Elohim', want to land at a secure embassy to be built for them close to Jerusalem. Their chief aim, says Raël, is to make us aware that it is also our destiny to create life on other planets.

He describes receiving the initial information at a series of face-to-face meetings after seeing a UFO land in a remote region of France. Two years later he says he was taken aboard a similar extra-terrestrial spacecraft and transported briefly to the planet of the Elohim. Since then at seminars on all five continents of the world he has been teaching meditation techniques which he says they gave him to prepare us for a future as extraordinary as their own.

The great prophets of all the world's major religions, he asserts, were similarly contacted by the Elohim at discreet meetings and each was given a message of guidance appropriate for his own era. But this, says Raël, is their *final* message which at long last allows us to replace belief with understanding.

If time proves Raël's claims to be true, the magnitude of what *The Final Message* purports to reveal could make it one of the most significant books of this or any other age.

THE
FINAL
MESSAGE

RAËL

THE TAGMAN PRESS
LONDON
London, Sydney, New York

THE FINAL MESSAGE

First publication (in paperback) in Great Britain 1998 by The Tagman Press
an imprint of Tagman Worldwide Limited
16 Hornton Street, Kensington,
London W 8 4NR
London, Sydney, New York

ISBN: 0 9530921 1 9

A CIP catalogue record for this book is available
from The British Library

Typeset by CGB, Lewes
Printed by MFP Design and Print
Longford Trading Estate, Thomas Street,
Stretford, Manchester M32 0JT

CONTENTS

CONTENTS

BOOK TWO

Extra-Terrestrials Took
Me to Their Planet

CONTENTS

Illustrations are on pages 105 to 108

PUBLISHER'S NOTE

The books written by Claude Raël following his claimed encounters with occupants of UFOs in southern France have been translated into some twenty five different languages during the past twenty years. Until now, the work of translation, publishing and distribution has been carried out privately in various countries by spare-time volunteer members of the International Raëlian Movement, which was set up by the author in the mid-1970s.

The Final Message is the first of Raël's books to receive commercial publication anywhere in the world. This re-titled English-language edition is a new re-translation of his two original French books – *Le Livre Qui Dit La Vérité – The Book Which Tells the Truth,* which first appeared in France in 1974, and *Les Extra-Terrestres M'ont Emmené Sur Leur Planète – Extra-Terrestrials Took Me to Their Planet,* which appeared in 1975.

A combined English-language hardcover edition of these two books was first printed by the International Raëlian Movement in Canada in 1978 entitled *Space Aliens Took Me to Their Planet.* The organisation printed a similar paperback English edition in Japan, beginning in 1986, under the title, *The Message Given to Me by Extra-Terrestrials.* In 1979 in France Raël published *Áccueillir Les Extra-Terrestres* and in 1980 *La Méditation Sensuelle.* English translations of these two books were also printed in Japan beginning in 1986 entitled respectively *Let's Welcome Our Fathers From Space* and *Sensual Meditation.*

In the intervening years since he first published the two books which make up *The Final Message* the author has previously added nothing to those original texts. But to give perspective to the impact these books have had since they first appeared, Raël has written a special postscript for this new English edition.

FOREWORD
by
Anthony Grey

THIS extraordinary book, I am convinced, contains revealed information of the greatest magnitude and importance for humanity. Written in simple, matter-of-fact terms, it provides what is for me the first truly persuasive explanation of our physical origins, our planetary history and our chronically divisive religious beliefs.

Above all it affirms that we are not alone in our universe – but it vastly overshadows everything else published in the UFO field by offering apparently authoritative insights into topics as diverse as the infinite nature of all living matter, genetics, human sexuality, sport, psychology, politics, criminality and even the significance of such mundane issues as property and marriage.

In asserting that all life forms on Earth including ourselves were genetically engineered by human scientists from another part of our galaxy, it demystifies and refocuses the ancient scriptures of all the world's major religions which I accept can now be seen to testify obscurely to this fact. Most controversially it abolishes the notion that a benevolent, knowing, all-powerful, spiritual God presides over us all.

The scriptures, it emphasises, are about representatives of that ultra-sophisticated civilisation – human beings just like ourselves – who care deeply about us because it was here that they first discovered and developed their own genius for transforming life from planet to planet by their mastery of DNA. In short this book sets our past, present and future on a firm scientific basis – but without, in my view, diminishing the beauty, joy and spirituality of our existence.

The author of these unique writings was born Claude Vorilhon in France in September 1946. He changed his name to Raël which means 'messenger' in Hebrew after seeing a flying saucer UFO land in a remote volcanic region of south central France in December 1973. During several meetings on successive days its human occupant verbally dictated most of the first half of this volume, saying it was 'a message to be addressed to all humanity'. He charged Raël with the mission of making its contents known worldwide and Raël rapidly wrote and published it himself in French under the title *The Book Which Tells the Truth*.

Nearly two years later, in October 1975, a second encounter occurred in woodland near Brantôme in the Périgord region of France. Raël describes this in the second section of the book entitled *Extra-Terrestrials Took Me to Their Planet*, which he also originally published as a separate volume in French.

In view of the fact that American and Russian astronauts have so far succeeded in venturing only into the nearest margins of space in orbit around the Earth and our moon, it perhaps seems outlandish at first sight to accept that without a spacesuit or any other special apparatus, Raël could have been whisked unexpectedly from a wooded European glade to another planet far across our galaxy. But this is what he describes, detailing many extraordinary experiences on the planet of his hosts who call themselves 'the Elohim'.

In recounting this brief outline of Raël's story I have not inserted any customary qualifying words such as 'alleged' or 'reported' which responsible journalists – and especially former foreign correspondents – might rightly be expected to employ to distance themselves from any controversial, unprovable information they are conveying. I've done this intentionally to underline my conviction that Raël is a man of integrity describing genuine experiences in a sincere and truthful fashion.

An international journalist is of course accustomed to assessing the reliability or otherwise of those he quotes for information, even when sometimes concealing his confidant's identity behind a stock phrase like 'a usually well-informed source'.

My estimation of Raël is that he is a reliable witness to what he has experienced, fantastic though it may seem. I think he is indeed 'a *uniquely* well-informed source' and, after hearing him lecture and after reviewing my own and other interviews with him, it is my impression that perhaps even now he is saying less than everything he learned during those extraordinary, unsought meetings in the mid-1970s. More importantly perhaps, the profound logic and rationality of what he was told by his interlocutor from another planet appears unassailable to me.

I interviewed Raël twice in preparing an investigative radio documentary series for the BBC World Service entitled 'UFOs – Fact, Fiction or

Fantasy?' I also interviewed sane, responsible Frenchmen who met and decided to support him during the period of his two extraordinary encounters in the 1970s and I have come to know and respect many other leading and rank-and-file members of his international organisation. In presenting Raël's story briefly to a world radio audience as just one aspect of the complex UFO phenomenon, I observed the time-honoured journalistic practice of impartial detachment – but here I have no hesitation in publicly declaring my conviction that Raël has written books of the utmost importance and significance for our understanding of ourselves and the universe in which we live.

If that is so, it is legitimate to ask, why are the contents of this book not universally known and accepted in the world some twenty-three years after they were first made public?

There was a sharp flurry of public interest in France after Raël announced the outline of what he had been told in a television interview programme as soon as he finished his first book. But somehow the remarkable story did not immediately gain widespread acceptance in Europe nor travel further abroad at that time along normal news channels.

So this, in my view, is a front-page, top-of-the-bulletin story which has never yet been given its due global prominence. If and when proven true, this body of information might well come to be described as the greatest revelation in mankind's recorded history. But of course there are two obvious reasons why it has not been quickly recognised as such.

Firstly, there is no incontrovertible, physical proof to back up what Raël has written. And secondly, the nature of what he says is deeply disturbing to the entrenched belief systems of religious, scientific, academic and other institutions all around the world.

As individuals too, we are all unconsciously influenced by the conventions of our education, our upbringing and the limited climate of thought produced by our largely unadventurous news media.

It requires considerable effort on the part of individuals to become independently open-minded and overcome such influences. For these reasons, this extraordinary information has seeped out only slowly around the world over the past twenty three years, largely through the steady, unspectacular efforts of the International Raëlian Movement which at the time of writing lays claim to some 40,000 members in more than eighty countries.

For more than twenty years Raël himself has, with gentle and patient good humour, explained his story again and again to radio, television and print journalists in most countries of the world. When mocked or derided in video recordings I have watched, he conducts himself always with the same unshakable confidence and never loses the demeanour of a man who knows he is telling the truth.

As far as providing proof is concerned, however, Raël quotes the Elohim as saying that they are deliberately withholding any physical evidence that would support his contentions – beyond the fact that their extra-terrestrial craft will appear more and more frequently in our skies as time goes by. It is otherwise important, they say, that we consider this information without proof. The logic and rationality of what they have revealed effectively contains its own hallmark of truth and whether or not we understand and accept their information and philosophical insights is a vital test of our intelligence. From how we react, they say, they will judge whether we are mature enough to be entrusted with their scientific knowledge which is 25,000 years in advance of our own.

They do not choose to land openly in any one country because that would involve violating national air space. Landing would also imply approval of that country's government and philosophy – and they do not so approve of any existing nation on Earth. Therefore they need an embassy of their own with the kind of extraterritorial rights enjoyed by any respected, visiting diplomat in a foreign state. Since their first embassy on Earth was Jerusalem's first temple, they have asked for this new embassy to be built as close as possible to that ancient city.

Yet the passage of time and the slowness with which this understanding is spreading around the world is also providing its own growing substantiation of what Raël has written. In 1974–75 when he first began to say that all life forms on Earth had been created in laboratories by Elohim scientists via their mastery of DNA, our own genetic research scientists were far less advanced in their work than they are today. In February 1997 the announcement of an historic global breakthrough in the field of biology was made from Edinburgh, revealing that British embryologists had succeeded in artificially cloning a sheep named Dolly.

The cloning of human beings, it was said, would become possible within two years and Raël promptly issued a press release saying: 'All this

12

demonstrates that the technology which was considered impossible at the time of my original revelations is now perfectly attainable'.

New advances in understanding DNA appear almost daily in our newspapers and in Tokyo a year or two earlier, Japanese scientists had announced that their research indicated that the gene pool for all races on Earth originated from a surprisingly small common base dating back approximately 13,000 years. This figure echoed what Raël had written with uncanny precision since the Elohim had said they began their work here 25,000 years ago and had spent some 12,000 years preparing the planet and creating the ecology, the marine and bird life and then land mammals before embarking finally on the creation of human beings 'in their own image'.

Raël says the Elohim leaders have been alive continually during those 25,000 years, having long since learned how to genetically recreate the human body with memory and personality intact. Soon, they contend, we will be able to expand our own average life span to around 1,000 years on our way to emulating them. Raël says they also monitor the thoughts and deeds of every individual on Earth by computer and can recreate each and any of us at will at the moment of death by a remote sampling of a single cell of our bodies. He reports that some 8,000 individuals from Earth had already been recreated on their planet when he was taken there. . .

But no brief summary can really do justice to the import of the book. The enormity of such assertions as those just mentioned requires that measured consideration be given to them in their context. Therefore my hope in writing this foreword is that others will be encouraged to give the whole book a careful reading. If it is all true, nothing could be more important.

The world of UFO research is awash with many amazing and often conflicting testimonies and claims, virtually all of them unprovable. What Raël has written does not reconcile all these conflicts in an instant – and nothing could.

Outside of the disturbing and still unexplained phenomenon of claimed abduction experiences which are being reported worldwide, other people have come forward over the past forty or fifty years to insist that they have had friendly personal contacts with extra-terrestrial visitors to our planet. This list of 'contactees' contains some fraudsters as well as others who are obviously sincere. But none of them has remotely approached Raël in the sheer scale of the information reportedly offered – and Raël is adamant that he alone has been entrusted with the truth.

It is just over five years at the time of writing since I first read the contents of this book myself. Presented with a copy by a French business executive whom I had met at a conference, I began reading it after getting into bed late one evening – and read on right through the entire night, never once sleeping then or even during the whole of the next day.

I was seized almost immediately by a feeling of awe that I had, by good fortune, stumbled across the greatest possible truths – and that feeling has never left me since.

After reflecting carefully on the book's enormous implications over the past five years, I now believe it also has the potential to transform us and our world beyond all present expectations.

At a purely practical level, if national leaders could take this book seriously and steel themselves to the thought that our world is a 'developing country' with many seemingly insoluble problems, and that unlimited aid and assistance is available from a generous, highly-advanced superpower living beyond our planet, then working towards an historic meeting at an extra-terrestrial embassy near to Jerusalem could be seen as a worthy and sensible international goal.

But much more important even than that I believe, is the book's core revelation about the very nature of the reality in which we live. Things infinitely small, the Elohim say, have exactly the same structure as things infinitely large – and they assured Raël they had proved this scientifically. This sounds incredible perhaps because our own science can not yet conceive of it, but they say that the atoms and sub-atoms in the cells of our bodies are mirror images of the universe above us; they contain minute planetary systems and galaxies on which complex, intelligent life forms like ourselves exist.

Similarly our own planet, galaxy and universe are tiny particles in an atom of some immense organic being and all matter at different levels mirrors itself in this way. Matter and time have no beginning and no end, they say, and everything is cyclic.

Interlocked Star of David triangles symbolising these fundamental truths – which are illustrated and explained in the selection of photographs printed in this book – were emblazoned on the first extra-terrestrial craft which landed before Raël's eyes in France. During his second encounter he was taught meditation techniques rooted in these understandings which he has been assiduously passing on ever since at seminars on all five continents of the world. Called 'sensual meditation' or 'meditation of all the senses', these techniques are designed to awaken the individual mind to its greatest potential by first fully awakening the physical sensibilities of the body.

The undoubted benefits of any kind of meditation are being recognised increasingly by the medical professions but the techniques taught by Raël specifically help individuals to feel a greater sense of harmony with the infinite nature of all things and consequently with each other. Beneficial chemical reactions are stimulated within the body, health is enhanced, mental and physical inner ease increases. In short what is unique about these teachings and practices is that they combine the spiritual with the scientific in a commonsense fashion, promising a transformation of society that begins where any real change must begin – with the individual.

In my view, for the many reasons outlined here, *The Final Message* marks the end of a long era of incomprehension and ignorance about ourselves and the purposes of our existence. I don't think its potential importance can be overstated: it is possibly the most important book to be published anywhere in the world for two thousand years. If it receives the attention it deserves, I believe it could herald and usher in an unprecedented epoch of worldwide enlightenment and change.

Summer 1997
London

Anthony Grey is a former foreign correspondent with Reuters in Eastern Europe and China and the author of the international best-selling historical novels *Saigon*, *Peking* and *Tokyo Bay*.

BOOK ONE

THE BOOK
WHICH TELLS
THE TRUTH

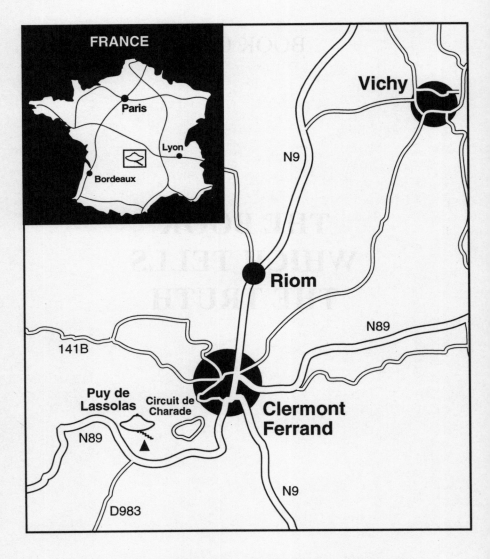

**Site of Raël's first encounter: Puy de Lassolas volcano, near
Clermont-Ferrand, 13 December 1973.**

1

THE ENCOUNTER

EVER since I was nine years old I have had but one passion – motor racing. I founded a specialist motor sport magazine in 1970, simply to be able to live in the environment of a sport where man is constantly trying to surpass himself while striving to surpass others. Since my early childhood I had dreamed of one day being a motor racing driver, following in the footsteps of someone as famous as Fangio. Thanks to contacts made through the magazine I founded, I was given the opportunity to race and about ten trophies now adorn my apartment as a result of those races.

On 13 December 1973, however, I went to a volcano overlooking Clermont-Ferrand in central southern France. I went more to get a breath of fresh air than to take a drive in my car. My legs were itching after a full year following the races from circuit to circuit, almost always living on four wheels, so to speak.

The air was cool at the time, and the sky rather grey with a background mist. I walked and jogged a little and left the path where my car was parked, aiming to reach the centre of the crater called Puy-de-Lassolas where I often went for picnics with my family in the summer.

What a superb and breathtaking place it was! To think that thousands of years ago, right where my feet were standing, lava had spurted out at incredibly high temperatures. Decorative volcanic 'bombs' can still be found among the debris. The stunted vegetation resembled that of Provence in France but without sunshine.

I was just about to leave and looked for the last time towards the top of the circular mountain, which was formed by an accumulation of volcanic slag. It reminded me how many times I had slid down those steep slopes, as if I were on skis. Suddenly in the fog, I saw a red light flashing; then a sort of helicopter was descending towards me. A helicopter, however, makes a noise but at that moment, I could hear absolutely nothing, not even the slightest whistle. A balloon maybe? By now, the object was about twenty metres above the ground, and I could see it had a somewhat flattened shape.

It was a flying saucer.

I had always believed in their existence, but I had never dreamed I would actually see one. It measured some seven metres in diameter, about 2.5 metres in height, was flat underneath and cone-shaped. On its underside, a very bright red light flashed, while at the top an intermittent white light reminded me of a camera flash cube. This white light was so intense, that I could not look at it without blinking.

The object continued to descend, without the slightest noise until it stopped and hovered motionless about two metres above the ground. I was petrified and remained absolutely still. I was not afraid, but rather filled with joy to be living through such a great moment. I bitterly regretted not having brought my camera with me.

Then the incredible happened. A trap door opened beneath the machine and a kind of stairway unfolded to the ground. I realised that some living being was about to appear, and I wondered what it was going to look like.

First two feet appeared, then two legs, which reassured me a little, since apparently I was about to meet a man. In the event, what at first I took to be a child came down the stairway and walked straight towards me.

I could see then this was certainly no child even though the figure was only about four feet (1.2 metres) tall. His eyes were slightly almond shaped, his hair was black and long, and he had a small black beard. I still had not moved and he stopped about ten metres away from me.

He wore some sort of green one-piece suit, which covered his entire body, and although his head seemed to be exposed, I could see around it a strange sort of halo. It was not really a halo but the air about his face shone slightly and shimmered. It looked like an invisible shield, like a bubble, so fine that you could barely see it. His skin was white with a slightly greenish tinge, a bit like someone with liver trouble.

He smiled faintly and I thought it best to return his smile. I felt rather ill at ease, so I smiled and bowed my head slightly in greeting. He answered with the same gesture. Thinking that I had to find out if he could hear me, I asked: 'Where do you come from?'

He answered in a strong, articulate voice that was slightly nasal: 'From very far away'.

'Do you speak French'? I enquired.

'I speak all the languages of the Earth.'

'Do you come from another planet?'

'Yes', he replied.

As he spoke, he moved closer and stopped about two metres from me.

'Is this the first time you have visited the Earth'?

'Oh no!'

'Have you been here often?'

'Very often – to say the least'.

'Why did you come here?'

'Today, to talk to you.'

'To me?'

'Yes, to you, Claude Vorilhon, editor of a small motor sport magazine, married and father of two children.'

'How do you know all that?'

'We have been watching you for a long time.'

'Why me?'

'This is precisely what I want to tell you. Why did you come here on this cold winter morning?'

'I don't know . . . I felt like walking in the fresh air . . .'

'Do you come here often?'

'In the summer yes, but almost never in this season.'

'So why did you come today? Had you planned this walk for a long time?'

'No. I don't really know. When I woke up this morning I suddenly had an urge to come here.'

'You came because I wanted to see you. Do you believe in telepathy?'

'Yes, of course, it's something I've always been interested in – as well as the subject of "flying saucers". But I never thought I'd see one myself.'

'Well, I used telepathy to get you to come here because I have many things to tell you. Have you read the Bible?'

'Yes, but why do you ask?'

21

'Have you been reading it for a long time?'

'No, as a matter of fact, I bought it only a few days ago.'

'Why?'

'I really don't know. Suddenly I had an urge to read it . . .'

'Again I used telepathy to make you decide to buy it. I have chosen you for a very difficult mission, and I have many things to tell you. So come into my craft where we can talk more comfortably.'

I followed him, climbing up the small staircase beneath the machine which, on closer inspection, looked more like a flattened bell with a full and bulging underside. Inside it two seats faced one another and the temperature was mild even though the door was still open.

There was no lamp, but natural light emanated from everywhere. There were no instruments like those you find in an aircraft cockpit. The floor was made of a sparkling alloy which was slightly bluish. The chairs were colourless and translucent, but very comfortable and made from one piece of material. I sat on the larger one that was set closer to the floor, so that the face of the little man sitting in front of me was at the same level as mine.

He touched a spot on the wall and the whole machine became transparent except for its top and bottom. It was like being in the open air, but the temperature was mild. He invited me to take off my coat, which I did, and then he started to speak.

'You regret not having brought your camera so that you could have talked about our meeting to the whole world – with proof in your hands?'

'Yes, of course . . .'

'Listen to me carefully. You will tell human beings about this meeting, but you will tell them the truth about what they are, and about what we are. Judging from their reactions we will know if we can show ourselves freely and officially. Wait until you know everything before you start speaking publicly. Then you will be able to defend yourself properly against those people who will not believe you and you will be able to bring them incontestable proof. You will write down everything I tell you and publish the writings as a book.'

'But why did you choose me?'

'For many reasons. First of all, we needed someone in a country where new ideas are welcomed and where it is possible to talk about such ideas openly. Democracy was born in France, and this country has a reputation the world over for being the country of freedom. Also we needed someone who is intelligent and quite open to everything. Above all we needed someone who is a free thinker without being anti-religious. Because you were born of a Jewish father and a Catholic mother, we consider you to be an ideal link between two very important peoples in the history of the world. Besides, your activities do not in any way predispose you to making incredible revelations, and this will make your words all the more believable. Since you are not a scientist, you will not complicate things and will explain them simply. Not being a literary man, you won't compose elaborate sentences which are difficult to read for a great many people. Finally, we decided to choose someone who was born after the first atomic explosion in 1945, and you were born in 1946. We have in fact been following you since your birth, and even before. This is why we have chosen you. Do you have any other questions?'

'Where do you come from?'

'From a distant planet about which I will tell you nothing for fear that men of the Earth might be unwise enough to disturb our peace.'

'Is your planet very far away?'

'Very far. When I tell you the distance you will understand that it is impossible to reach it with your present level of scientific and technical knowledge'.

'What are you called?'

'We are people like you, and we live on a planet similar to Earth.'

'How long does it take you to come here?'

'As long as it takes to think about it.'

'Why do you come to Earth?'

'To monitor and watch over the development of humanity. Human beings on Earth are the future, we are the past.'

'Are there many people on your planet?'

'There are more people than on yours.'

'I would like to visit your planet. Can I?'

'No. First of all you couldn't live there because the atmosphere is different from yours, and you have not been trained for such a journey.'

'But why meet here?'

'Because the crater of a volcano is an ideal place, away from irksome people. I shall leave you now. Come back tomorrow at the same time with the Bible and something to take notes with. Do not bring any metallic object and speak to no one of our conversation, otherwise we will never meet again.'

He handed me my coat, let me climb down the ladder and waved his hand. The ladder folded up and the door closed without a sound. Still without making the slightest murmur or any whistling sound, the craft rose gently to a height of about 400 metres, then disappeared into the mist.

2

THE TRUTH

Genesis

THE following day I was at the meeting place again as arranged with a notebook, a pen and the Bible. The flying machine reappeared on time and I found myself face to face once more with the little man who invited me to enter the machine and sit in the same comfortable chair.

I had spoken to nobody about all this, not even to my closest friends and he was happy to learn that I had been discreet. He suggested I take notes and then he started to speak.

'A very long time ago on our distant planet, we had reached a level of technical and scientific knowledge, comparable to that which you will soon reach. Our scientists had started to create primitive, embryonic forms of life, namely living cells in test tubes. Everyone was thrilled by this.

The scientists perfected their techniques and began creating bizarre little animals but the government, under pressure from public opinion, ordered the scientists to stop their experiments for fear they would create monsters which would become dangerous to society. In fact one of these animals had broken loose and killed several people.

Since at that time, interplanetary and intergalactic explorations had also made progress, the scientists decided to set out for a distant planet where they could find most of the necessary conditions to pursue their experiments. They chose Earth where you live. Now I would like you to refer to the Bible where you will find traces of the truth about your past. These traces, of course, have been somewhat distorted by successive transcribers who could not conceive of such high technology and could therefore only explain what was described as being a mystical and supernatural force.

Only the parts of the Bible that I will translate are important. Other parts are merely poetic babblings of which I will say nothing. I am sure you can appreciate that, thanks to the law which said that the Bible had always to be recopied without changing even the smallest detail, the deepest meaning has remained intact throughout the ages, even if the text has been larded with mystical and futile sentences.

So let us start with the first chapter of the Book of Genesis:

In the beginning Elohim created the heaven and the earth. *Genesis 1: 1.*

"Elohim", translated without justification in some Bibles by the word "God", means in Hebrew "those who came from the sky" and furthermore the word is a plural. It means that the scientists from our world searched for a planet that was suitable to carry out their projects. They "created", or in reality discovered the Earth, and realised it contained all the necessary elements for the creation of artificial life, even if its atmosphere was not quite the same as our own.

And the spirit of Elohim moved across the waters. *Genesis 1: 2.*

This means the scientists made reconnaissance flights and what you might call artificial satellites were placed around the Earth to study its constitution and atmosphere.

The Elohim saw that the light was good. *Genesis 1: 4.*

To create life on Earth it was important to know whether the sun was sending harmful rays to the Earth's surface and this question was fully researched. It turned out that the sun was heating the Earth correctly without sending out harmful rays. In other words the "light was good".

There was a night and there was a morning, the first day. *Genesis 1: 5.*

This research took quite some time. The "day" mentioned here corresponds to the period in which your sun rises under the same sign on the day of the vernal equinox, in other words, about 2,000 years on Earth.

He divided the waters under the heavens from the waters above the firmament. *Genesis 1: 7.*

After studying the cosmic rays above the clouds the scientists descended below the clouds but stayed above the waters. That means they were between the clouds, "the waters above the firmament", and the ocean covering the whole planet, "the waters under the heavens".

Let the waters under the heavens be gathered together into one place and let dry land appear. *Genesis 1: 9.*

After they studied the surface of the ocean they studied the sea bed and determined that it was not very deep and fairly even everywhere. So then, by means of fairly strong explosions which acted rather like bulldozers, they raised matter from the bottom of the seas and piled it up into one place to form a continent.

Originally there was on Earth only one continent and your scientists have recently acknowledged that all the continents, which have drifted apart over many years, used to fit perfectly into one another to form one land mass.

Let the earth grow vegetation, grass and trees which have in them their own seed according to their species. *Genesis 1: 11.*

In this magnificent and gigantic laboratory, they created vegetable cells from nothing other than chemicals which then produced various types of plants. All their efforts were aimed at reproduction. The few blades of grass they created had to reproduce on their own.

The scientists spread out across this immense continent in small research teams. Every individual created different varieties of plants according to their inspiration and the climate. They met up at regular intervals to compare their research and their creations. The people back on their own planet followed their progress from afar with passion and amazement. The most brilliant artists came and joined the scientists in order to give some plants purely decorative and pleasing roles, either through their appearance or their perfume.

Let there be lights in the heavens to separate the day from the night, and let them be used as signs for the seasons, for the days and for the years. *Genesis 1: 14.*

By observing the stars and the sun they could measure the duration of the days, the months and the years on Earth. This helped them regulate their life on the new planet – so different from their own where days and years did not have the same duration. Research in astronomy enabled them to locate themselves precisely and to understand the Earth better.

Let the waters teem with an abundance of living animals, and let the birds fly above the Earth. *Genesis 1: 20.*

Next they created the first aquatic animals, from plankton to small fish, then very large fish. They also created seaweed to balance this little world, so that the small fish could feed on it and the bigger fish could eat the small fish in turn.

Thus a natural balance would be established, and one species would not destroy another species in order to survive. This is what you now refer to as "ecology" and that was achieved successfully. The scientists and artists met often and organised competitions to determine which team had created the most beautiful or most interesting animals.

After the fish they created birds. This was done under pressure, it must be said, from the artists, who went out of their way to create the most stunning forms with the craziest colours. Some of them had great trouble flying because their beautiful feathers were very cumbersome. The contests went even further, embracing not only physical characteristics but also the behaviour of these animals, particularly the wonderful dances of their mating rituals.

Some other groups of scientists created frightful animals, veritable monsters, which proved right those people who had opposed the creation plans on their own planet. These were dragons, or what you call dinosaurs and brontosaurs.

Let the living animals emerge from the earth according to their species: livestock, reptiles, wild animals, according to their species. *Genesis 1: 24.*

After marine organisms and birds, the scientists created land animals on a planet where the vegetation had by now become magnificent. There was plenty of food for the herbivores. These were the first land animals which were created. Later they created carnivores to balance the herbivorous population. Here too, the species had to maintain equilibrium. Those scientists who did all this came from the same planet as me. I am one of those people who created life on Earth.

It was at that time that the most skilful among us wanted to create an artificial human being like ourselves. Each team set to work and very soon we were able to compare our creations. But on our home planet people

28

were outraged when they heard that we were making "test tube children" who might come to threaten their world. They feared that these new human beings could become a danger if their mental capacities or powers turned out to be superior to those of their creators. So we had to agree to leave the new humans to live in a very primitive way without letting them know anything scientific, and we made our own actions mystifying to them. It is easy to work out how many teams of creators did this – each race on Earth corresponds to a team of creators.

Let us make man in our own image after our likeness: let them have authority over the fish of the sea and the birds of the sky, over the livestock, over all wild animals and over all the reptiles which crawl on the earth. *Genesis 1: 26.*

"In our image!" You can see that the resemblance is striking. That is when the trouble started for us. The team located in the country you now call Israel, which at the time was not far from Greece and Turkey on the original continent, was composed of brilliant creators who were perhaps *the* most talented team of all.

Their animals were the most beautiful and their plants had the sweetest perfumes. This was what you call "paradise on Earth". The human beings they created there were the most intelligent. So steps had to be taken to ensure that they did not surpass their creators. The created, therefore, had to be kept in ignorance of the great scientific secrets while being educated for the purpose of measuring their intelligence.

Of every tree in the garden you may eat, but of the tree of good and evil you shall not eat of it, for on the day that you eat of it, you shall die. *Genesis 2: 17.*

This means you – the created – can learn all you want, read all of the books that we have here at your disposal but never touch the scientific books, otherwise you will die.

He brought to man all the animals to see what he would call them. *Genesis 2: 19.*

Human beings had to have a thorough understanding of the plants and animals living around them, their way of life, and the way to get food from them. The creators taught them the names and the powers of everything that existed around them since botany and zoology were not considered dangerous for them. Imagine the joy of this team of scientists, having two children, a male and a female running around, eagerly learning what was being taught to them.

The serpent . . . said to the woman . . . of the fruit of the tree which is in the midst of the garden . . . you would not die, for Elohim know that on the day you eat thereof, your eyes will be opened and you shall be as gods. *Genesis 3: 1–5.*

Some scientists in this team felt a deep love for their little human beings, their "creatures", and they wanted to give them a complete education in order to make them scientists like themselves. So they told these young people who were almost adults that they could pursue their scientific studies and in so doing they would become as knowledgeable as their creators.

Then the eyes of them both were opened and they knew that they were naked. *Genesis 3: 7.*

The new human beings then understood that they could also become creators in their turn and they became angry at their "parents" for having kept them away from scientific books, considering them to be like dangerous laboratory animals.

Yahweh Elohim said to the serpent: be damned . . . on your belly you shall crawl and dust you shall eat all the days of your life. *Genesis 3: 14.*

The "serpent" was this small group of creators who had wished to tell the truth to Adam and Eve and as a result they were condemned by the government of their own planet to live in exile on Earth, while all the other scientists had to put a stop to their experiments and leave the Earth.

Elohim made for the man and his wife coats of skin and clothed them. *Genesis 3: 21.*

The creators gave their creations the basic means of survival, enough to manage without needing any further contact with them. The Bible has preserved a sentence which is close to the original document:

Now that man has become one of us, thanks to science . . . Now we must ensure that he does not put out his hand to take from the "tree of life", eat and live forever. *Genesis 3: 22.*

Human life is very short but there is a scientific way to prolong it. Human scientists who study all their lives can only begin to amass sufficient knowledge to start making interesting discoveries when they get old, which is the reason why human progress is so slow. If humans could live ten times longer, scientific knowledge would take a gigantic leap forward.

If when they were first created these new beings could have lived much longer, they would have quite rapidly become our equals because their mental faculties are slightly superior to our own. They are unaware of their full potential. This applies especially to the people of Israel who, as I mentioned earlier, had been selected in a contest as the most successful type of humanoid on Earth due to their intelligence and genius. This explains why they have always considered themselves to be the "chosen people". In truth they were the people chosen by the teams of scientists who gathered together to judge their creations. You can see for yourself the number of geniuses born out of that race.

So he drove out man and placed at the East of the garden of Eden the Cherubim and a flaming sword which turned every way to guard the way to the tree of life. *Genesis 3: 24.*

Soldiers with atomic disintegration weapons were placed at the entrance to the creators' residence to prevent human beings from stealing more scientific knowledge.'

The Flood

'LET us move on to the fourth chapter of *Genesis.*

And in the process of time it came to pass that Cain brought of the fruit of the ground to Elohim, and Abel also brought the firstlings of his flock. *Genesis 4: 3–4.*

The creators in exile who were left under military surveillance, urged the human beings to bring them food in order to show their own superiors that the newly created people were good, and that they would never turn against their creators. Thus they managed to obtain permission for the leaders of these first human beings to benefit from the "tree of life", and this explains how they lived so long: Adam lived for 930 years, Seth for 912 years and Enos for 905 years, and so on as is stated in *Genesis,* Chapter 5, verses 1–11.

When men began to multiply on the face of the earth, and daughters were born unto them, the sons of Elohim saw the daughters of men were beautiful. They took them as wives of all they had chosen. *Genesis 6: 2.*

The creators living in exile took the most beautiful daughters of humanity and made them their wives.

My spirit shall not always strive with man for he is also flesh, yet his days shall be one hundred and twenty years. *Genesis 6: 3.*

Longevity is not hereditary and much to the relief of the authorities on the distant planet, the children of the new human beings did not automatically benefit from the "tree of life". Thus the secret of life was lost, and mankind's progress was slowed down.

When the sons of Elohim came into the daughters of men and had children by them, they were the heroes of old, men of renown. *Genesis 6: 4.*

There you have proof that the creators could have intercourse with the daughters of humanity whom they had created in their own image, and in so doing produced exceptional children. These actions seemed very dangerous to people on the distant planet. The scientific progress on Earth was fantastic and they decided to destroy what had been created.

And Yahweh saw that man had done much evil on earth and that his thoughts and inclinations were always evil. *Genesis 6: 5.*

The "evil" in question was the desire of human beings to become scientific and independent people equal to their creators. Being "good", as far as those on the Elohim's planet were concerned, meant the new human beings would remain primitive, vegetating on the Earth. Their "evil" was their wish to progress, perhaps enabling them one day to catch up with their creators.

The government then decided from their distant planet to destroy all life on Earth by sending nuclear missiles. However when the exiled creators were informed of the project they asked Noah to build a spaceship which would orbit the Earth during the cataclysm containing a pair of each species that was to be preserved.

This was true figuratively speaking, but in reality – and your scientific knowledge will very soon enable you to understand this – a single living cell of each species, male and female, is all that is required to recreate a whole being. This is something like the first living cell of a foetus in the womb of its mother which already possesses all the information needed to create a human being right down to the colour of its eyes and hair. This was a colossal task but it was completed on time.

When the explosion took place, life had already been preserved a few thousand kilometres above the Earth. The continent was submerged by a gigantic tidal wave which destroyed all forms of life on its surface.

The ark was lifted above the Earth. *Genesis 7: 17.*

As you can clearly see, it is said that the ark was lifted "above" the Earth and not "on" the water.

Then it was necessary to wait until there was no more dangerous radioactive fallout:

The waters grew above the Earth during one hundred and fifty days. *Genesis 7: 24.*

The spacecraft had three sections:

You shall build it in stages, the lower, the second, and the third. *Genesis 6: 16*

Later it landed on Earth and, besides Noah, it carried a couple from each race of human beings on the Earth.

Elohim remembered Noah . . . a wind blew across the Earth and the waters became still. *Genesis 8: 1*

After monitoring the level of radioactivity and dispersing it scientifically, the creators told Noah to release the animals to see if they could survive in the atmosphere. This operation was successful and they were able to venture out into the open air. The creators then asked the human survivors to work and multiply, and show their gratitude to their benefactors who had created them and saved them from destruction. Noah agreed to give a portion of their harvest and their cattle to the creators to ensure they survived.

Noah built an altar for Elohim and took all the pure beasts and all the pure birds, and he made an offering on the altar. *Genesis 8: 20.*

The creators were happy to see that humans wished them well and they promised never to try to destroy their creation again. They understood that it was only normal for them to want to progress scientifically.

Every inclination of man's heart is evil. *Genesis 8: 21.*

Each race of humanity was then returned to its original place of creation and each animal was recreated from the cells which had been preserved aboard the ark.

From them came the separated nations on earth after the flood. *Genesis 10: 32.'*

The Tower of Babel

'BUT the most intelligent race, the people of Israel, were making such remarkable progress that they were soon able to undertake the conquest of space with the help of the exiled creators. The latter wanted their new human beings to go to the creators' planet to obtain their pardon, by showing that they were not only intelligent and scientific but also grateful and peaceful. So they built an enormous rocket – The Tower of Babel.

And now they have decided to do this, henceforward nothing they plan to do will be beyond their reach. *Genesis 11: 6.*

The people on our planet became frightened when they heard about this. They were still observing the Earth and knew that life had not been destroyed.

Let us go down there and confuse their speech, so that they will not understand what they say to one another. So Yahweh scattered them from there all over the earth. *Genesis 11: 7.*

So they came and took the Jews who had the most scientific knowledge and scattered them all over the continent among primitive tribes in countries where nobody could understand them because the language was different and they destroyed all their scientific instruments.'

Sodom and Gomorrah

'THE exiled creators were pardoned and allowed to return to their original planet where they pleaded the case of their magnificent creation. As a result everyone on the distant planet fixed their eyes on the Earth because it was inhabited by people they had themselves created.

But among the humans who had been dispersed on Earth, a few nursed the desire for vengeance, so they gathered in the towns of Sodom and Gomorrah and, having managed to salvage a few scientific secrets, they prepared an expedition aimed at punishing those who had tried to destroy them. Consequently the creators sent two spies to investigate what was going on.

And there came two angels to Sodom in the evening. *Genesis 19: 1.*

Some humans tried to kill them but the spies managed to blind their attackers with a pocket atomic weapon:

And they smote them with blindness, both small and great. *Genesis 19: 11.*

They warned those who were peaceful to leave the town because they were going to destroy it with an atomic explosion.

Leave this place: for Yahweh is going to destroy the city. *Genesis 19: 14.*

As the people were leaving town, they were in no particular hurry because they did not realise what an atomic explosion could mean.

Flee for your lives; do not look back and do not stop anywhere. *Genesis 19: 17.*

And the bomb fell on Sodom and Gomorrah.

Then Yahweh rained down fire and brimstone from the skies of Sodom and Gomorrah. He overthrew those cities and destroyed all the plain, and all inhabitants of the cities, and that which grew upon the ground. But Lot's wife looked back and she became a pillar of salt. *Genesis 19: 24–26.*

As you now know, burns caused by an atomic explosion kill those who are too near and make them look like salt statues.'

The Sacrifice of Abraham

'LATER, after most of their leading intellectuals had been destroyed and they had relapsed into a semi-primitive state, the creators wished to see if the people of Israel, and particularly their leader, still had positive feelings towards them. This is related in the paragraph where Abraham wants to sacrifice his own son. The creators tested him to see if his feelings towards them were sufficiently strong. Fortunately the experiment ended positively.

Do not raise your hand against the boy; do not touch him. Now I know that you fear Elohim. *Genesis 22: 12.*

There you have it. Assimilate it all and write down everything I have just told you. I will tell you more tomorrow.'

Once again the small man took leave of me and his spacecraft rose slowly into the air. Because the sky was clearer this time I was able to watch more closely as it took off. It hovered motionless at a height of about 400 metres, then still without the slightest sound, the vessel turned red as if it was heating up, then as white as white-hot metal, and then finally a sort of bluish purple like an enormous spark which was impossible to look at. Then it disappeared completely.

3

WATCHING OVER
THE CHOSEN PEOPLE

MOSES. THE TRUMPETS OF JERICHO. SAMSON THE TELEPATHIST.
THE FIRST RESIDENCE. ELIJAH THE MESSENGER. THE MULTIPLICATION OF BREAD.
THE FLYING SAUCERS OF EZEKIEL. THE LAST JUDGEMENT. SATAN.
HUMANITY COULD NOT UNDERSTAND.

Moses

THE next day I again met with my visitor and he immediately continued his story.

'In *Genesis,* Chapter 28, there is another description of our presence:

A ladder which rested upon the ground with its top reaching to heaven, and the angels of Elohim were going up and down upon it. *Genesis 28: 12.*

Because of the destruction of centres of progress such as Sodom and Gomorrah and the elimination of the most intelligent individuals, human beings had lapsed back into a primitive state and had begun, rather stupidly, to adore pieces of stone and idols, forgetting those who had really created them.

Put away the strange gods that are among you. *Genesis 35: 2.*

In *Exodus* we appeared to Moses.

And the angel of Yahweh appeared unto him in a flame of fire out of the midst of a bush, and behold, the bush burned with fire and, the bush was not consumed. *Exodus 3: 2.*

A rocket landed in front of him, and his description corresponds to what a Brazilian tribesman might say today if we were to land before him in a flying vessel illuminating the trees without burning them.

The people chosen as the most intelligent had lost their most brilliant minds and had become slaves to neighbouring tribes who were more numerous since they had not undergone the same destruction. It was thus necessary to restore dignity to the people of Israel by returning their land to them.

The beginning of *Exodus* describes all that we had to do to help liberate the people of Israel. Once freed, we guided them to the country which we had destined for them.

And Yahweh went before them by day in a pillar of a cloud, to lead them the way, and by night in a pillar of fire, to give them light, to go by day and night. *Exodus 13: 21.*

In order to slow down the march of the Egyptians who had started to pursue them:

The pillar of the cloud went before their face and stood behind them . . . and it was a cloud and darkness to one side, but it gave light by night to the other. *Exodus 14: 19–20.*

The smoke emitted behind the people of Israel made a curtain which slowed down their pursuers. Then the crossing of the water was made possible by a repulsion beam which cleared a passageway:

And made the sea dry land, and the waters divided . . . Thus Yahweh saved Israel. *Exodus 14: 21 and 30.*

While they were crossing the desert the chosen people began to feel hungry:

Upon the face of the wilderness fine flakes appeared, fine hoarfrost on the ground. *Exodus 16: 14.*

The manna was nothing more than pulverised synthetic chemical food which, when spread on the ground, swelled with the early morning dew.

As for the staff which allowed Moses "to draw water from the rock" as it says in *Exodus 17: 6* – it was nothing but a detector of underground water pools similar to those which you use at present to find oil for example. Once the water is located, one has only to dig.

Then in Chapter 20 of *Exodus* a certain number of rules are cited.

Because the Israelites were so primitive they needed laws regarding morals and especially hygiene. These were outlined in the commandments.

The creators came to dictate these laws to Moses on Mount Sinai, and they arrived in a flying vessel.

There were thunders and lightnings, and thick cloud upon the Mount, and the voice of a trumpet exceedingly long . . . And Mount Sinai was altogether in smoke because Yahweh descended upon it in fire: and the smoke thereof ascended as the smoke of a furnace and the whole mount quaked greatly. And the voice of the trumpet sounded long and waxed louder and louder. *Exodus 19: 16–19.*

The creators were afraid of being invaded or maltreated by human beings. It was therefore essential that they be respected, even venerated, so that they would be in no danger.

The people cannot come up Mount Sinai . . . but let not the priests and the people break through to come unto Yahweh for fear that he may break out against them. *Exodus 19: 23–24.*

Also it was written:

And Moses alone shall come near Yahweh: but the elders of Israel and the people may not go up with him at all. *Exodus 24: 2.*

They saw the God of Israel:

Under his feet there was, as it were, a pavement of sapphire, clear blue as the heavens. *Exodus 24: 10.*

There you have the description of the pedestal upon which one of the creators presented himself, and it was made of the same bluish alloys as the floor of the machine in which we are now sitting.

And the sight of the glory of Yahweh was like the devouring fire on the top of the Mount. *Exodus 24: 17.*

Here you have a description of "the glory" – in reality the flying vessel – and, as you have already noticed, upon take-off it has a coloration similar to fire.

This team of creators was going to live on the Earth for some time and they wished to eat fresh food. That is why they asked the Israelites to bring them fresh provisions regularly, and also riches which they wanted to take back to their own planet. I suppose you might call it colonisation.

You shall accept whatever contribution each man shall freely offer. This is

what you shall accept: gold, silver, copper, violet, purple and scarlet yard. *Exodus 25: 2–4.*

They also decided they would like to live more comfortably so they asked the human beings to build them a residence according to plans they had drawn up. The plans are described in Chapter 26 of the *Book of Exodus.* In this residence they would meet the representatives of the people. It was a meeting place where people brought food and gifts as a pledge of submission.

He entered the tent of the meeting place . . . When Moses entered it, the pillar of cloud came down and stayed at the entrance to the tent while Yahweh spoke with Moses . . . And Yahweh would speak to Moses face to face, as one man speaks to another. *Exodus 33: 8–11.*

Just as today I can speak to you as you can speak to me, man to man.

My face you cannot see, for no man may see me and live. *Exodus 33: 20.*

There you have reference to the difference in atmosphere between our planets. Humans cannot see their creators unless the latter are protected by a pressurised suit, because the terrestrial atmosphere is not suitable for them. If you came to our planet you would see the creators without a space suit, but you would die because the atmosphere is not suitable for you.

The entire beginning of *Leviticus* explains how the foods offered to the creators had to be brought to them. For example in *Leviticus 21: 17* it says:

No man among your descendants for all time who has any physical defect shall come to present food to his God . . .

This is obviously to prevent sick or deformed people, who were symbols of failure and therefore unbearable to the eyes of the creators, from presenting themselves before them.

In the *Book of Numbers, 11: 7–8* there is a very precise description of the manna which your chemists could very easily produce.

And the manna looked like coriander seed, the colour of gum resin . . . the taste of it was as the taste of fresh oil.

This manna was nothing more than a chemical food but the creators preferred fresh fruits and vegetables.

They will bring unto Yahweh the first ripe fruits of all produce in their land. *Numbers 18: 13.*

Later the creators taught human beings how to inject themselves to treat snake bites.

Make a fiery serpent and set it upon a pole so that anyone bitten could look at it and live. *Numbers 21: 8.*

As soon as someone was bitten he "looked" at the "serpent of brass", that is to say a syringe was brought to him so that he could be injected with serum.

Finally, the journey which led the "chosen people" to the promised land came to an end. Following the advice of the creators they destroyed the idols of the local primitive people and took over their territories.

You will destroy all their melted metal statues . . . and you will possess the country. *Numbers 33: 52–53.*

The "chosen people" finally reached their promised land.

Because he loved your fathers he has chosen your race after them. *Deuteronomy 4: 37.*

In the *Book of Joshua* Chapter 3, Verse 15, we read about the crossing of the Jordan.

When the priests carrying the Ark reached the Jordan . . . the water coming down from upstream was brought to a standstill. It piled up like a bank for a long way back . . . the waters were completely cut off and the people crossed over opposite Jericho.

Thus the creators helped the "chosen people" cross without getting their feet wet just as they had done in their escape from the Egyptians, by using the same water repulsion ray.'

The Trumpets of Jericho

'AT the end of Chapter 5 in the *Book of Joshua,* there is a meeting between a military creator and the chosen people regarding the resistance of the city of Jericho.

I am here as captain of the army of Yahweh. *Joshua 5: 14.*

A military consultant was sent to the Jewish people to assist them in the siege of Jericho. It is easy to understand how the walls were knocked down. You know that the very high voice of a singer can crack a crystal glass. By using highly amplified supersonic waves one can knock down a brick wall. This is what was done, using a very complicated instrument which the Bible calls a "trumpet".

> When they make a long blast with the ram's horn, and when you hear the sound of the trumpet ... the walls of the city shall fall down flat. *Joshua 6: 5.*

At a given moment the supersonic waves were emitted in a synchronised way and the walls fell down. A little later some real bombing took place.

> Yahweh hurled great hailstones at them out of the sky and more died from the hailstones than the Israelites slew by the sword. *Joshua 10: 11.*

This full scale bombing, as indicated, killed more people than the swords of the Israelites. One of the most misunderstood passages is in *Joshua,* Chapter 10, Verse 13, where it is stated:

> So the sun stood still, and the moon halted until the people had avenged themselves upon their enemies.

This simply means that it was a flash war which lasted only one day – in fact it is stated later that the war occupied "nearly a whole day". It was so short, when you consider the extent of the land conquered, that people thought the sun had stood still.

In the *Book of Judges,* Chapter 6, Verse 21, one of the creators is again in contact with a man called Gideon who continues to supply him with food.

> The angel of Yahweh put forth the end of the staff that was in his hand, and touched the flesh and the unleavened cakes: and there rose up fire out of the rock and consumed the flesh and the unleavened cakes. Then the angel of Yahweh departed out of his sight.

The creators were unable to eat in the open air because of their pressurised suits, but if necessary, using a scientific technique, they could feed themselves by extracting the essentials from these offerings using a flexible tube, or cane. The process radiates flames, which made people at the time think sacrifices to God were being made.

In Chapter 7 of the *Book of Judges,* 300 men with "trumpets" surrounded the enemy camp and, using amplified supersonic instruments, they blew them simultaneously in order to drive all the people in the camp mad. You know now that certain high pitched sounds carried to extremes, can drive anyone mad.

Indeed the soldiers who had been surrounded went wild, fought among themselves, and ran away.'

Samson the Telepathist

'IN *Judges*, Chapter 13, there is yet another example of mating taking place between the creators and human women:

And the angel of Yahweh appeared unto the woman and said: You are barren and have no child, but you shall conceive and give birth to a son. *Judges 13: 3.*

It was necessary that the fruit of this union be healthy so that the behaviour of the child could be studied. This is why he tells her:

And drink not the wine nor strong drink, and eat not any unclean thing, for lo, thou shall conceive and bear a son. And no razor shall come on his head, for the child shall be a Nazarene consecrated unto God from the womb. *Judges 13: 4–5.*

Later it is written:

And the angel of Elohim came again to the woman who was sitting in the fields; her husband was not with her. *Judges 13: 9.*

It is easy to imagine what happened during her husband's absence . . . It was an easy task for the scientists to cure her sterility. In this way she was made aware that she was going to give birth to an exceptional individual, and that she should take the utmost care of her baby. It was wonderful for the creators to mate with a daughter of humanity. This enabled them to have sons ruling directly on Earth, where the atmosphere was not suitable for themselves.

The point about not shaving off any hair is very important. The human brain is like a huge transmitter, capable of sending out a multitude of very accurate waves and thoughts. In fact, telepathy is nothing more than that. But this type of transmitter requires antennae, and the hair and beard are these antennae. That is why you should not shave off any hair if you want to make use of your transmitters. You have surely noticed that many of your scientists have long hair, and often a beard. Prophets and other wise people have them, too. Now you can understand why.

The child was born. It was Samson, whose story you know. He was able to communicate directly with "God" by telepathy, thanks to his natural antennae, his hair. And the creators could then help him during difficult moments and produce marvels to reinforce his authority.

But when Delilah cut his hair he could no longer ask for help. Then his eyes were gouged out by his enemies, but when his hair grew again, he regained his "strength". That is to say, he could once again ask for help from the creators who then demolished the temple where he was touching the columns. All of this was attributed to Samson's strength.

In *Samuel* Chapter 3, we find Elijah initiating Samuel into telepathy. The creators wanted to contact Samuel and he thinks that Elijah is speaking to him. He "hears voices".

Go lie down: and it shall be, if he calls thee, that thou shalt say: speak Yahweh for thy servant heareth. *1 Samuel 3: 9.*

This is a little like the behaviour of amateur radio operators who might say, "Go ahead, I can hear you loud and clear". And the telepathic conversation begins:

Samuel, Samuel . . . And Samuel answered: Speak for thy servant heareth. *1 Samuel 3, 10–11.*

In the episode where David challenges Goliath there is quite an interesting sentence which ends:

. . . that he should defy the armies of the living God? *1 Samuel 17: 26.*

This shows the reality of the presence in that epoch of a quite tangible "God".

Telepathy as a means of communication between the creators and human beings was only possible when the Elohim were in proximity to the Earth. When they were on their distant planet, or elsewhere, they could not communicate in this way.

For this reason they set up a transmitter-receiver which was transported in the "Ark of God", an apparatus containing its own atomic powered cell. This is why in the *First Book of Samuel*, Chapters 5 and 6, when the Philistines stole the Ark, their idol Dagon lay face down on the ground nearby as the result of an electrical discharge caused by their clumsy mishandling of it.

They also suffered radiation burns from the dangerous radioactive materials:

And he afflicted them with tumours. *1 Samuel 5: 6*

Even the Hebrew people who had not taken precautions while handling the Ark were harmed:

The oxen stumbled and Uzzah reached out to the Ark of God and took hold of it. Yahweh was angry with Uzzah and struck him down for his rash act. So he died there beside the Ark of God. *2 Samuel 6: 6–7.*

The Ark almost fell over and Uzzah, trying to hold it up, touched a dangerous part of the machine and was electrocuted.

In the First Book of Kings (1 Kings 1: 50 and 1 Kings 2: 28) we read in several places of individuals who "caught hold on the horns of the altar." This refers to the manipulation of the transmitter-receiver levers which was necessary when trying to communicate with the creators.'

The First Residence to Welcome the Elohim

'THE great King Solomon built a sumptuous residence to welcome the creators when they came to visit the Earth.

Yahweh said he resides in a cloud. I truly construct a house for you. *1 Kings 8: 12–13.*

The glory of Yahweh has filled the house of Yahweh. *1 Kings 8: 11.*

The cloud filled the house of Yahweh. *1 Kings 8: 10.*

I shall reside among the sons of Israel. *1 Kings 6: 13.*

So the creators lived in a cloud, or rather in a vessel that orbits above the clouds. Imagine trying to make primitive people understand that.

A man of God sent by Yahweh, came from Judah to Bethel . . . He said . . . the altar will be split apart. Jeroboam stretched his hand from the altar and said "seize him!" But the hand he stretched out . . . shrivelled up so he could not pull it back and the altar split apart. *1 Kings 13: 1–5.*

With the help of an atomic disintegrator, one of the creators destroyed the altar and burned the hand of the man who did not show respect for the creators. He returns to one of the Elohim's terrestrial camps by another route to keep their whereabouts secret.

Do not return again by the same way that thou camest. So he went by another way. *1 Kings 13: 10.*

44

In *1 Kings*, Chapter 17, verse 6 there is an example of the radio control of animals through the use of electrodes, as you yourselves are beginning to discover.

And the ravens brought him bread and flesh in the morning, and bread and flesh in the evening.

At this time following some of their own new discoveries, the creators decided to appear less frequently. They wanted to give human beings the opportunity to develop by themselves in order to see if they would reach the age of scientific knowledge unaided. So, the creators began to use increasingly discreet means of communicating with humans – as in the method of feeding Elijah using "homing" ravens.

This was the beginning of a gigantic experiment throughout the galaxy in which several humanities are in competition. The creators decided to appear less often, while at the same time reinforcing the authority and reputation of their ambassadors – the prophets – by using miracles. That is to say, scientific means which were then incomprehensible to the people of that era:

**Look, your son is alive . . . Now by this I know that thou art a man of God.
*1 Kings 17: 23–24.***

Elijah had healed a young child who was dying. Later he ordered two bull calves to be placed on logs at Mount Carmel, one to be consecrated to the idol Baal, and the other to the creators. The one that would ignite by itself would represent the one true "God".

Obviously, at a moment agreed upon in advance between Elijah and the creators, the Elohim's chosen log burst into flames, even though the wood was wet. This was accomplished by a powerful beam similar to a laser, emitted from a vessel hidden in the clouds:

Then the fire of Yahweh fell and consumed the whole offering, and the wood, and the stones, and the dust, and licked up the water that was in the trench. *1 Kings 18: 38.*[9]

Elijah the Messenger

'THE creators paid particular attention to Elijah.

An angel touched him and said: "Arise and eat". At his bedside was a

pancake ... and a jar of water. All this happened in the desert ... *1 Kings 19: 5–6.*

And behold Yahweh passed by, and a great and strong wind rent the mountains, and broke the rocks in front of Yahweh. But Yahweh was not in the wind. And after the wind came an earthquake but Yahweh was not in the earthquake; and after the earthquake came a fire but Yahweh was not in the fire; and after the fire a still small voice. *1 Kings 19: 11–12.*

There you have the exact description of a landing by a machine similar to one of your rockets. Then further on, a vision of the creators is described.

I saw Yahweh sitting on his throne and all the army of heaven standing by him. *1 Kings 22: 19.*

The creators once again used telepathy – this time group telepathy – so that none of the prophets could predict the truth to the King:

I will be a lying spirit in the mouths of all his prophets. *1 Kings 22: 22.*

In the *Second Book of Kings,* there is further evidence of the protection which the creators gave to Elijah:

If I am a man of God, may fire fall from heaven and consume you and your company! Fire fell from heaven and consumed the officer and his fifty men. *2 Kings 1: 12.*

This operation happened again, but the third time:

The angel of Yahweh said unto Elijah: go down with him and be not afraid of him. *2 Kings 1: 15.*

In the *Second Book of Kings,* Chapter 2, Elijah is invited onto a space-craft which takes off with him on board:

When Yahweh would take up Elijah into heaven by a whirlwind. *2 Kings 2: 1.*

Also later it adds:

There appeared a chariot of fire and a horse of fire, which parted them both asunder and Elijah went up by a whirlwind into heaven. *2 Kings 2: 11.*

This is a clear description of a spacecraft taking off and when the narrator speaks of horses of fire, he is referring to the fire and the smoke which were emitted from the blast pipes. If you showed certain South American or African tribespeople a rocket taking off, they would be incapable of

46

understanding this scientific phenomenon in a rational way, and would look upon it as something supernatural, mystical, and divine. When returning to their tribes, they would speak of fire horses and chariots.

Further on in the *Second Book of Kings* Chapter 4, verses 32–7 Elisha, like his father, performs a resurrection. He heals and brings back to life a child who was dead. This happens quite frequently nowadays when mouth to mouth resuscitation and heart massage revives a person whose cardiac muscle has ceased to function.

Then Elisha proceeds to multiply the bread.'

The Multiplication of Bread

'A man . . . brought the man of God twenty barley loaves . . . but his ser-ant said: How can I feed one hundred people with twenty loaves . . . Elisha said . . . They will eat and there will be some left over. So he set it before them and they ate and left some over, as Yahweh had said. *2 Kings 4: 42–44.*

The creators had brought synthetic dehydrated food with them, which when added to water, increased to five times its original volume. So with twenty small loaves of bread there was enough food for a hundred people.

You are already familiar with the little vitamin pills which nourished your first astronauts. They take up very little space but contain all the necessary nutritional elements. One pill is enough to feed one person. A quantity equivalent in volume to one small loaf of bread is enough to feed five people. Therefore twenty loaves are sufficient to feed one hundred people.

But the people of Israel had begun adoring metal idols; they had also become cannibals and were completely immoral, much to the disgust of their creators:

So was Israel carried away out of their land. *2 Kings 17: 23.*

That was the beginning of the dispersion of the Israelites whose civilisation, instead of making progress, was constantly regressing in contrast to their neighbours who took advantage of their opportunities.

In the *Book of Isaiah* you again find:

In the year of King Uzziah's death I saw the Lord seated on a throne, high and exalted . . . above him stood the seraphim: each one had six wings, one pair covered their faces, and one pair their feet, and one pair was spread in flight. *Isaiah 6: 1–2.*

That is a description of the creators dressed in their one piece space suits fitted with six small jet engines, two on their backs, two on their arms, and two on their feet, all for steering purposes.

Listen, a noise on the mountains like that of a great multitude! An uproar among kingdoms like nations amassing together! Yahweh is mustering an army for war. They come from far away lands from the ends of heaven. Yahweh and his instruments of wrath to destroy the land. *Isaiah 13: 4–50.*

The whole truth is encapsulated in that quote, it is just a matter of reading between the lines in order to understand. *They come from far away lands, from the ends of heaven.* That could not be more clear.

You thought in your own mind, I will ascend to heaven. I will raise my throne above the stars of God. *Isaiah 14: 13.*

This refers to the human scientists who had accumulated sufficient knowledge to undertake a trip to the creators' planet but were destroyed at Sodom and Gomorrah. The army of the heavens is described here at that time, when they arrived with the weapons of wrath to destroy the whole country. It was those human scientists of Sodom and Gomorrah who said:

I will rise above the cloud banks and will equal myself to the most high. *Isaiah 14: 14.*

But the destruction prevented humans from equalling their creators, "the most high":

He made the world a wilderness. *Isaiah 14: 17.*

The nuclear explosion is described further on:

For a cry is gone round the border of Moab; the howling thereof unto Eglaim and unto the well of Beer-elim . . . for the waters of Dimon are filled with blood . . . *Isaiah 15: 8–9.*

A few were saved because they sheltered in bunkers.

Go my people, enter your rooms and shut your doors behind you; withdraw a brief while until the wrath has gone by. *Isaiah 26: 20.*

The Flying Saucers of Ezekiel

'IT is in the *Book of Ezekiel,* Chapter One, beginning at verse 4, that we find the most interesting description of one of our flying machines.

I looked, and saw a windstorm coming out of the north, an immense cloud

with flashing lightning and surrounded by brilliant light. The centre of the fire looked like glowing metal and in the fire was what looked like four living creatures. In appearance their form was that of a man, but each had four faces and four wings. Their legs were straight, their feet were like those of a calf and gleamed like burnished bronze. Under their wings on their four sides they had the hands of a man. All four of them had faces and wings, and their wings touched one another. Each one went straight ahead; they did not turn as they moved.

Their faces looked like this: each one had the face of a man, and on the right side each had the face of a lion, and on the left the face of an ox; each also had the face of an eagle. Such were their faces. Their wings were spread upwards; each had two wings one touching the wing of another creature on either side, and two wings covering its body. Each one went straight ahead. Wherever the spirit would go they would go, without turning as they went.

The appearance of the living creatures was like burning coals of fire, like torches. Fire moved back and forth among the creatures; it was bright and lightning flashed out of it. The creatures sped back and forth like flashes of lightning.

As I looked at the living creatures, I saw a wheel on the ground beside each creature with its four faces. This was the appearance and structure of the wheels. They sparkled like chrysolite, and all four looked alike. Each appeared to be made like a wheel intersecting a wheel. As they moved they would go in any one of four directions the creatures faced; the wheels did not turn about as the creatures went. Their rims were high and awesome and all four rims were full of eyes all around. When the living creatures moved, the wheels beside them moved; and when the living creatures rose from the ground, the wheels also rose. Wherever the spirit would go, they would go, and the wheels would rise along with them, because the spirit of the living creature was in the wheels. When the creatures moved they also moved; when the creature stood still, they also stood still; and when the creatures rose from the ground, the wheels rose along with them, because the spirit of the living creatures was in the wheels.

Spread out above the heads of the living creatures was what looked like an expanse, sparkling like ice and awesome. Under the expanse their wings were stretched out one towards the other, and each had two wings covering its body. When the creatures moved, I heard the sound of their wings, like the roar of rushing waters, like the voice of the Almighty, like the tumult of an army. When they stood still, they lowered their wings.

Then there came a voice from above the expanse over their heads as they stood with lowered wings. Above the expanse over their heads was what looked like a throne of sapphire, and high above on the throne was the figure like that of a man. *Ezekiel 1: 1–26.*

There you have a description which could not be more precise of the landing of the creators in their flying machines. The "windstorm" is the trace of smoke or vapour trail that present-day planes leave behind them at high altitudes. Then the machine appeared with its blinking light, the "flashing lightning" and "glowing metal". Later, four creators appear wearing antigravity suits with small directional jet engines attached. These are described as the "wings" on their metal suits and "their feet . . . gleamed like burnished bronze". You have surely noticed how shiny the suits of your astronauts are.

As for the "flying saucers" or "wheels", their appearance and their operation were not at all badly described considering it is a primitive person who is speaking. "As it were a wheel in the middle of a wheel . . . they turned not when they went".

In the centre of the flying saucer, very similar to the one in which we are now sitting, was the habitable section, the rim. "All four rims were full of eyes, all round". In the same way that our clothing has evolved and we no longer wear those cumbersome space suits, our vessels then had portholes – the "eyes" around the rims – because we had not then discovered how to see through metallic walls by modifying their atomic structure at will.

The flying saucers stayed near the creators ready to help them if the need arose, since they were loading supplies and carrying out routine maintenance on the large intergalactic vessel above them. Other creators inside the vessels were directing them. "The spirit of the living creature was in the wheels". This is quite clear.

The suit described with its four portholes was similar to your first diving suits. "Each of them had four faces . . . and they did not turn as they moved".

The smaller saucers were something like your own LEMs – lunar excursion modules – small, short range vehicles used for exploratory missions. Above them the larger interplanetary vessel waited.

Spread out above the heads of the living creatures was what looked like an expanse, sparkling like ice and awesome . . . Above the expanse over

their heads was what looked like a throne of sapphire, and high above the throne was a figure like that of a man. *Ezekiel 1. 26*

The latter individual on the large vessel, was supervising and co-ordinating the movements of the creators.

Frightened by all this Ezekiel fell flat on his face because those mysterious events had to come from no one other than "God". But one of the creators said to him:

Son of man stand up and let me talk with you . . . Listen to what I say . . . eat what I give you. *Ezekiel 2: 1 and 7–8.*

This is an image, like the eating from the scientific tree of good and evil. It was intellectual food that he was given. In this case it was a book.

Then I saw a hand stretched out to me holding a scroll . . . it was written all over on both sides.

There was writing on both sides, a very surprising thing at that time when usually only one side of parchment was written on.

Then the scroll is "eaten". This means that Ezekiel absorbed its meaning. What he learned is what you are learning now about humanity's origins. It was so exciting and comforting that he said:

So I ate it, and it tasted as sweet as honey. *Ezekiel 3: 3.*

Then Ezekiel is transported in the creators' vessel to the place where he was to spread the good news.

Then the spirit lifted me up . . . and I heard behind me a loud rumbling sound. *Ezekiel 3: 12.*

Further on the prophet is transported once again by the creators' flying machine:

The spirit lifted me up between the earth and the heaven, and in visions of God he took me to Jerusalem. *Ezekiel 8: 3.*

Ezekiel noticed afterwards that beneath their "wings" the cherubims had hands like humans:

And there appeared in the cherubims the form of a man's hand under their wings. *Ezekiel 10: 8.*

While I watched, the cherubims spread their wings and rose from the ground and as they went the wheels went with them. *Ezekiel 10: 19.*

Then the spirit lifted me up, and brought me . . . *Ezekiel 11: 1.*

51

The glory of Yahweh went up from the midst of the city, and stopped above the mountain which was on the east side of the city. Afterwards the spirit took me up and brought me . . . into Chaldea. *Ezekiel 11: 23–24.*

There you have some of the many journeys of Ezekiel in the creators' flying machines. Later another experience is described:

Yahweh set me down in the middle of the valley which was full of bones. *Ezekiel 37: 1.*

And there a miracle happens. The creators go on to resurrect human beings whose only remains are their bones.

As mentioned earlier, each cell of a living being contains all the information to reconstruct it completely. All you have to do is place a single cell, for example from bone remains, in a machine which provides all the living matter required to reconstruct that original being.

The machine supplies the matter, and the cell supplies all the required information, just as a spermatozoon contains all the information necessary to create a living being in the first place, right down to the colour of the hair and eyes.

Son of man, can these bones live? . . . There was a noise, and behold a shaking . . . the sinews and the flesh came up upon them, and the skin covered them . . . they came to life and stood upon their feet, an exceeding great army. *Ezekiel 37: 3–10.*

All this is very easy to do and you will do it some day. This is the origin of the ancient rituals in which elaborately protective sepulchres were built to bury great people so that one day they may be brought back to life everlasting. This is part of the secret of the "tree of life" – the secret of eternity.

In Chapter 40 Ezekiel is again carried away in a spacecraft which takes him into the presence of someone wearing a space suit:

He took me there . . . and set me upon a very high mountain, on whose south side were some buildings that looked like a city . . . and behold, there was a man whose appearance was like bronze . . . *Ezekiel 40: 2–3.*

This "city" is one of the Earth bases that the creators used at that time. They were always located on very high mountains so that the creators would not be disturbed by humans. The man "whose appearance was like bronze" is, of course, wearing a metallic suit. Similarly, due to our small stature, we were often mistaken for children or cherubs.

The priests in serving the creators in their terrestrial residence – the temple visited by Ezekiel – wore aseptic clothing when performing their duties, and those clothes always had to remain in the temple, to avoid being contaminated by germs dangerous to the creators:

When the priests have entered the holy place, they shall not enter the outer court without leaving behind the garments they have worn while performing their duties, for these are holy. *Ezekiel 42: 14*

They should have written, "for these garments are pure or sterile", but that was incomprehensible for primitive people who deified all that was told or shown to them at that period.

In *Ezekiel* Chapter 43, the big vessel, respectfully called "the glory of God", approached.

And I saw the glory of the God of Israel coming from the east. His voice was like the roar of rushing waters; and the land was radiant with his glory. *Ezekiel 43: 2.*

The creators did not want to be disturbed so they issued a directive:

This gate is to remain shut, it shall not be opened, and no man shall enter by it; because Yahweh, God of Israel, has entered in by it, therefore it shall be shut. *Ezekiel 44: 2.*

Only a "prince" is allowed to come and speak with the creators:

The prince himself is the only one who may sit inside the gateway to eat in the presence of Yahweh. *Ezekiel 44: 3.*

But the prince had to pass through a chamber where he was disinfected by special rays.

He shall enter by way of the porch of that gate and shall go out the same way. *Ezekiel 44: 3.*

The Levite priests were there to look after the creators.

They shall come near to me to minister unto me, and they shall come before me to offer unto me the fat and the blood . . . and they shall come near to my table, to minister unto me . . . *Ezekiel 44: 15–16.*

The odour of human perspiration was unpleasant to the creators:

When they enter the gates of the inner court, they must be clothed with linen garments . . . they shall not gird themselves with anything that causeth sweat. *Ezekiel 44: 17–18.*

There is a description also of how the Elohim's supply of fresh products continued.

The best of all your first fruits . . . and the first of your dough you will give to the priests so a blessing may rest on your household. *Ezekiel 44: 30.*

In Chapter 3 of the *Book of Daniel,* King Nebuchadnezzar condemned three men to the stake for refusing to worship a metal god instead of the creators. But the three men, who knew of the creators' existence, were saved by one creator who came to their aid in the glowing fire, armed with a repellent and refrigerative ray. He protected them from the heat and the flames with this and allowed them to walk away totally unscathed.

I see four men loose, walking in the midst of the fire, and they have no hurt; and the form of the fourth looks like a son of the gods. *Daniel 3: 25.*

Further on Daniel is cast into the lions' den but the lions do not harm him. There again, nothing too complicated was involved, just a paralysing beam to give enough time to get Daniel out of the den unharmed.

My God has sent his angel to shut the lion's mouth. *Daniel 6: 22.*

In the tenth chapter of *Daniel* you will find another interesting description of a creator.

I looked up and saw a man . . . his body gleamed like topaz, his face shone like lightning, his eyes flamed like torches, his arms and feet sparkled like a disc of bronze; and when he spoke his voice sounded like the voice of a multitude. *Daniel 10: 5–6.'*

The Last Judgement

'IF the Hebrew people were dominated by the Persians and Greeks it was because of their lack of faith. Consequently the Elohim punished the Hebrews by sending some of their "angels" amongst the Persians and Greeks to help those nations to progress technologically.

This explains the great moments in the history of those two civilisations. The archangel Michael was the leader of the delegation which was helping the Persians.

Michael, one of the chief princes, came to help the kingdom of Persia. *Daniel 10: 13.*

In Chapter 12 of *Daniel* the resurrection is again mentioned:

And many of them that sleep in the dust of the earth shall awake, some to everlasting life, and some to shame and everlasting contempt. *Daniel 12: 2.*

The "Last Judgement" will enable great individuals to live again. Those people who have acted positively for humanity and who have truly believed in their creators and followed their commandments will be welcomed with great joy by the people of the era when this will happen.

On the other hand, all the wicked people will feel shame before their judges and will live in eternal regret as an example for the rest of humanity:

The wise leaders shall shine like the bright vault of heaven and those who have guided the people on the true path shall be like the stars for ever and ever. *Daniel 12: 3.*

The geniuses will be the most highly esteemed, and the most highly rewarded. Those just individuals who allowed the geniuses to blossom, or the truth to triumph, will also be rewarded.

But you Daniel, keep the words secret and seal the book till the time of the end; many will seek here and there and knowledge shall be increased. *Daniel 12: 4.*

These words will only be understood when humanity has reached a sufficient level of scientific understanding – that is to say now. All this will happen:

When the power of the holy people ceases to be dispersed. *Daniel 12: 7.*

This will be when the people of Israel recover their land after their long Diaspora. The state of Israel was created a few decades ago, at the same time as the explosion of humanity's scientific knowledge.

Go your way, Daniel, for the words are kept secret and sealed till the time of the end. *Daniel 12: 9.*

All this could not be understood at that time. Now it can all be understood. In recent years scientific progress and the beginning of space exploration by human beings have been such that everything seems possible for humanity. Nothing now surprises people for they are used to seeing many wonders happening before their eyes on television. They can learn without astonishment that they really are made in the image of "God", their almighty creator, even as far as their scientific abilities are concerned. These days, miracles have become comprehensible.

In *Jonah*, the big fish that swallows the prophet is very interesting indeed. Jonah was thrown into the water from a small boat:

Now Yahweh had prepared a great fish to swallow up Jonah, and Jonah was in the belly for three days and three nights. *Jonah 1: 17.*

The "great fish" was in fact, a submarine as you know such vessels now. But for the people of that time it could only be a great fish, even though the gastric juices of such a fish would have digested a man quickly without any hope of his returning to the open air. What is more, Jonah would have needed air to breathe . . . In the submarine the creators were able to carry on a conversation with Jonah, to learn about the political developments of those times.

And Yahweh spoke unto the fish, and it vomited out Jonah upon the dry land. *Jonah 2: 10.*

The submarine came close to the shore and Jonah was back on land. In *Zechariah* Chapter 5, there is another description of a flying machine:

I looked up again and saw a flying scroll, twenty cubits (9 metres) long and ten cubits (4.5 metres) wide. *Zechariah 5: 1–2*

A little further on women amongst the creators appear for the first time:

Behold, there came out two women, and the wind was in their wings like the wings of a stork . . . *Zechariah 5: 9.*

These two female companions were accompanying the creators and both were equipped with autonomous flying suits when they appeared before Zechariah.

In *Psalms* 8, verse 5 it is said of human beings:

Thou hast made them a little less than the Elohim.

Human beings are virtually as strong intellectually as their creators. Those who copied out the texts did not dare write "equal" to the Elohim as it had been originally dictated.

His rising is at one end of the heavens, and his circuit touches their far-thest ends. *Psalms 19: 6.*

The creators came from a planet very far away from the Earth's orbit.

In the heavens he has pitched a tent for the sun. *Psalms 19: 4.*

Here is another allusion to the mass of earth which was created to form the original continent when the oceans covered the Earth.

Yahweh looks out from heaven and watches all mankind; he surveys from his dwelling place all the inhabitants of earth. *Psalms 33: 13–14.*

The creators watch humanity's behaviour as they always have done from their flying vessels.'

Satan

'IN the *Book of Job*, Chapter 1, you have the explanation of Satan:

Now there was a day when the sons of Elohim came to present themselves before Yahweh, and Satan also came with them. *Job 1: 6.*

Elohim in Hebrew literally means "those who come from the sky." The "sons of Elohim", in other words, the creators who watch human beings, report regularly to their planet of origin, indicating for the most part that human beings venerate and love the Elohim. But one of these Elohim, called Satan, was part of a group which had always condemned the creation of other intelligent beings on a planet as close as the Earth, seeing them as a possible threat. That is why, on seeing Job's devotion, which was one of the best examples of human beings loving their creators, he said:

Has not Job good reason to fear Elohim? . . . But stretch out your hand and strike all that he has, and then he will curse you to your face. And Yahweh said to Satan: so be it, all that he has is in your hands; only Job himself you must not touch. *Job 1: 9–12.*

Hearing Satan's assertion that had Job not been rich, he would not have loved his creators, the government gave full power to Satan to ruin Job. It would then be seen if he still venerated his creators, and that is why killing him was forbidden.

On seeing Job's dedication to respecting his creators, even when he was ruined, the government triumphed over the opposition, Satan. But Satan retorted that though Job had lost many things, he was still in good health. So the government gave Satan *carte blanche* so long as he did not kill Job.

He is in your hands but save his life. *Job 2: 6.*

Again, in the *Book of Job*, a small sentence in Chapter 37 is very interesting:

Can you beat out the vault of the skies, as he does, as hard as a mirror of cast metal? *Job 37: 18.*

In other words, are human beings capable of making "vaults of the skies"– in reality flying metallic vessels? People of that time thought it was possible for no one but God. And yet today it can be done.

Finally in view of Job's humility, the creators healed him and gave him back his wealth, his children and his health.'

Humans Could Not Understand

'IN the *Book of Tobit* in the Apocrypha, one of the creators' robots named Raphael also came to test humanity's reaction towards their creators.

Once he had accomplished his mission he left, after proving who he was:

> Everyday, I appeared unto you but neither did I eat nor drink . . . I am ascending to him who sent me. Write down these things that have happened to you. *Tobit 12: 19–20.*

All of this is easy to see in the writings. But once again you must try to understand.

> I shall tell you what wisdom is, and what is her origin, and I will not hide from you the mysteries of Elohim, but will reveal from the beginning of her birth, and bring the knowledge of her to light, and will not pass over the truth. *Wisdom of Solomon 6: 22.*

When the time comes "wisdom", the science which allowed all this to happen, will be understood by humanity. The Biblical writings will be proof of all this.

> For the greatness and beauty of created things give us a corresponding idea of their creators. *Wisdom of Solomon 13: 5.*

So it is simple to see the truth, recognising the creators by observing their creations.

> And who by these good things that are seen could not understand him that is. *Wisdom of Solomon 13: 1.*

To avoid being disturbed by humans the creators built their bases on high mountains where we now find traces of great civilisations (in the Himalayas and Peru, for example) as well as at the bottom of the sea. Gradually the mountain stations were abandoned in favour of submarine bases less accessible to humans. The creators who had been banished at the outset had hidden themselves in the oceans.

> In that day Yahweh with his cruel and mighty sword shall punish Leviathan that runaway serpent; and he shall slay the dragon that is in the sea. *Isaiah 27: 1.*

At that time the government of their planet wanted to destroy those who had created the humans.

It was not easy to see clearly among all those wonders, so of course the creators were deified and made into something abstract because human beings were unable to understand scientific facts.

And the book is delivered to him that is not learned, saying: Read this, I pray thee. But he said I am not learned. *Isaiah 29: 12.*

For a long time, humanity has held the truth in its hands but could not understand until it was sufficiently evolved scientifically to decode it.

Every man is brutish in his lack of knowledge . . . *Jeremiah 10: 14.*

Science enabled the creators to create and will enable human beings to do the same.

Yahweh possessed me in the beginning of his way, before his work of old. I was set up from everlasting, from the beginning, or ever the earth was . . . When he prepared the heavens I was there . . . When he gave to the sea his decree that the waters should pass his commandment . . . then I was with him as one brought up with him. And I was daily his delight, rejoicing always before him; rejoicing in the habitable parts of his earth, and my delights were with the sons of men. *Proverbs 8: 22–23, 27, 29–31.*

Intelligence and science, these are the two virtues that enabled the creators to create the land mass – the single continent – and the living beings they placed upon it. And now this intelligence and this spirit leads the human brain to repeat the acts of their creators.

Since the beginning of time it has been so, people create other people like themselves on other planets. The cycle continues. Some die, others take over. We are your creators and you will create other humanities.

That which has been is now; and that which is to be, already has been. *Ecclesiastes 3: 15.*

The animals were also created and will be recreated. Just like human beings, no more, no less. The species that disappear will live again when you know how to recreate them.

Yea, they all have one breath; so that man has no pre-eminence above the beast, for all is vanity. Ecclesiastes 3: 19.

We, the creators, will only show ourselves officially if humanity is grateful to us for having created them. We fear that human beings might hold a grudge against us – which we cannot accept.

We would like to begin making open contact with you and give you the benefit of our considerable advance in scientific knowledge – so long as we could be sure that you would not turn against us, and that you would love us as your parents.

Woe to him who quarrels with his maker. Will the clay ask the potter what he is making or his handiwork say to him that you have no skill? Woe unto him that says to his father, what are you begetting? *Isaiah 45: 9–10.*

Fear of not being loved by human beings has led your creators to allow you to progress scientifically by yourselves, with almost no help.

The emblem you see engraved on this machine and on my suit represents the truth. It is also the emblem of the Jewish people, the Star of David, which means: "That which is above is like that which is below" and in its centre is the swastika which means that everything is cyclic, the top becoming the bottom, and the bottom in turn becoming the top. The origins and destiny of the creators and human beings are similar and linked.

Do you not know? Have you not heard? Were you not told from the beginning? Have you not understood from the foundation of the earth? *Isaiah 40: 21.*

The traces of the creators' bases on high mountains is mentioned in the *Book of Amos*

He who ... marches over the heights of the earth. *Amos 4: 13.*

The creators had seven bases in all:

Those seven, they are the eyes of Yahweh ... which run to and fro throughout the whole world. *Zechariah 4: 10.*

This is the origin of the seven branched candlestick, the meaning of which has been lost. In the beginning at the creators' headquarters, there was a switchboard with seven lighted switches enabling them to stay in contact with the other bases and with the interplanetary vessel orbiting the Earth. In *Psalms 139: 4–6* there is an allusion to telepathy:

Before a word is on my tongue you know it completely, O Yahweh, you hem me in behind and before; you have laid your hand on me. Such knowledge is too wonderful for me; it is high, I cannot attain it.

At that time telepathy was unimaginable, hence "such knowledge is too wonderful for me". Astronomy and interplanetary journeys were also unthinkable at the time.

He numbers the stars one by one and calls each by name. Great is our Lord, and great his power: his understanding is infinite. *Psalms 147: 4–5.*

Human beings were also unable to understand telecommunication.

He sends his command to the end of the earth, and his word runs swiftly. *Psalms 147: 15.*

We now reach a decisive turning point in the creators' work. They decided at that period to let humanity progress scientifically without ever intervening directly. They understood that they themselves had been created in the same way, and that by creating similar beings to themselves, they were allowing the cycle to continue.

But first, in order for the truth to be spread throughout the world they decided to send a Messiah who would be able to communicate worldwide what the people of Israel were then the only ones to know. This was in preparation for the day when the original mystery would be explained in the light of scientific progress – that is to say, the revelation. So they announced him:

But out of you, Bethlehem, shall come a governor for Israel, and whose roots are far back in the past, in days gone by . . . He shall stand and be their shepherd in the strength of Yahweh . . . to the ends of the Earth, and he shall be a man of peace. *Micah 5: 2–5.*

Exult, daughters of Jerusalem, here is your King coming forth to you . . . humble and carried on a mule . . . he will dictate peace to the nations, his empire will cover from sea to sea. *Zechariah 9: 9–10.*'

4

THE ROLE OF CHRIST

THE CONCEPTION. THE INITIATION. PARALLEL HUMANITIES.
SCIENTIFIC MIRACLES. DESERVING THE INHERITANCE.

The Conception

THE next morning we met again at the same spot and my host said:

'Christ's role was to spread the truth of the Biblical scriptures through-out the world so that they could serve as proof for all of humanity when the age of science would finally explain everything. The creators therefore decided to arrange for a child to be born of a woman of the Earth and one of their own people. The child in question would thereby inherit certain telepathic faculties which humans lack.

She was found with child of the Holy Ghost. *Matthew 1: 18.*

Mary was the woman chosen and obviously her fiancé found these tidings hard to accept but:

Behold the angel of the Lord appeared unto him. *Matthew 1: 20*

One of the creators appeared to explain that Mary would bring forth a son of "God". The prophets who were in contact with the creators, came from very far away to see the divine child. One of the spacecraft guided them:

We observed the rising of his star, and we have come to pay him homage . . .
And the star which they had seen at its rising went ahead of them until it
stopped above the place where the child lay. *Matthew 2: 2 and 9.*

62

The creators watched over the child:

And the angel of the Lord appeared in a dream to Joseph, saying arise and take the child and his mother, and flee into Egypt, and remain there until I tell you, for Herod will seek the child to destroy him. *Matthew 2: 13.*

The king was not too happy about the child-king who had just been born on his territory as the prophets had predicted. But after King Herod died, the creators told Jospeh that he could return to Israel.

When Herod was dead, an angel of the Lord appeared in a dream to Joseph in Egypt . . . saying: Arise and take the child and his mother, and go into the land of Israel, for those who sought the child's life, are dead. *Matthew 2: 19–20.*'

The Initiation

'WHEN he came of age, Jesus was led to the creators so that they could reveal to him his true identity, introduce him to his father, reveal his mission and make known to him various scientific techniques.

Heaven opened up; and he saw the spirit of God descending like a dove to alight upon him; and a voice from heaven was heard, saying: This is my son, my beloved, on whom my favour rests . . . Jesus was then led away by the spirit into the wilderness to be tempted by the devil. *Matthew 3: 16–17 and 4: 1.*

The devil, "Satan", the creator of whom we spoke previously, was always convinced that nothing good can come of humanity on Earth. He was "Satan the sceptic" and he was supported by the government's opposition on our distant planet.

So he tested Jesus to find out if his intelligence was positive and if he really loved and respected his creators. Having discovered that they could place complete confidence in Jesus, Jesus was allowed to go and accomplish his mission.

In order to rally people to him, Jesus performed "miracles" which, in reality, were the application of scientific teachings shown to him by the creators.

Sufferers from every kind of illness were all brought to him, and he cured them. *Matthew 4: 24.*

Blessed be the poor in spirit. *Matthew 5: 3.*

This sentence has been incorrectly interpreted as: "the poor are blessed". But the original meaning was that if the poor have spirit, then they will be happy – which is totally different.

Then Jesus told his apostles that they must spread the truth throughout the world. In the prayer called the "Lord's Prayer" or the "Our Father", the truth is stated literally:

Thy kingdom come . . . thy will be done on earth as it is in heaven. *Matthew 6: 10.*

In "heaven", on the creators' planet, the scientists eventually became the ruling group and then created other intelligent beings. The same thing will happen on Earth. The torch will be taken up again.

This prayer, which has been repeated time and again without anyone understanding its profound meaning, now takes on its full significance: "*On earth, as it is in heaven*".

Amongst other things, Jesus had been taught to speak convincingly through a type of telepathic group hypnosis:

And it came to pass when Jesus had finished these words, that the crowds were astonished at his teachings . . . for he was teaching them as one having authority, and not as their scribes . . . *Matthew 7: 28–29.*

He continued to heal the sick with the help of the creators who directed concentrated beams from a distance:

A leper approached him . . . Jesus stretched out his hand, touched him and said, Be clean again. And his leprosy was cured immediately. *Matthew 8: 2–3.*

And he did the same for a man who was completely paralysed. The operation was carried out from a distance using a concentrated ray, something like a laser, which burns only one spot through several layers.

Arise and walk . . . and he rose. *Matthew 9: 6–8.*

Further on in the *St Matthew's Gospel*, Jesus announced his mission:

I did not come to invite virtuous people, but sinners. *Matthew 9: 13.*

He did not come for the people of Israel, who knew of the existence of the creators, but rather so that this knowledge would be spread throughout the rest of the world.

Later there were more "miracles" somewhat similar to the first ones, all of which were medical. Nowadays there are transplants of hearts and other organs; leprosy and other similar illnesses are cured, and people are brought out of a coma with appropriate care. These would be considered miracles by technologically primitive people. At that time human beings were primitive and the creators were similar to people of your present "civilised" nations, although a little more advanced scientifically.

Further on we find an allusion to the creators among whom is Jesus' real father:

Whoever then will acknowledge me before men, I will acknowledge him before my father who is in heaven. *Matthew 10: 32.*

"Before my father who is in heaven" – this says it all. In fact "God" is not intangible or immaterial. He is "in heaven". This is obviously incomprehensible to people who at the time believed that the stars were attached to a heavenly canopy just like pretty light bulbs, all rotating around the centre of the Earth. Now since the advent of space travel and an understanding of the immensity of the universe, the old texts are brought to light in a comletely different way.'

Parallel Humanities

'IN *St. Matthew's Gospel,* Chapter 13, there is an important passage where Jesus explains in a parable how the creators left their planet to create life on other worlds.

The sower went out to sow. . .. And as he sowed, some seeds fell by the wayside, and the birds came and ate them up. . . And other seeds fell upon rocky ground, where they had not much earth . . . and when the sun rose they were scorched. . . Other seeds fell among thorns which grew up and choked the plants . . . And other seeds fell upon good ground, and yielded fruit, some a hundred fold, some sixty fold and some thirty fold. . . He who has ears to hear, let him hear. *Matthew 13: 3–9.*

All this is an allusion to the various attempts to create life on other planets – and three of them failed.

The first failed because of the birds which came and ate the seeds. In fact this was a failure caused by the proximity of the planet in question to the creators' original planet. Those who were against the creation of people similar to themselves saw a possible threat in the experiment and therefore went to destroy the creation.

The second attempt was made on a planet too near a sun which was too hot; therefore their creation was destroyed by noxious radiations.

The third attempt was made "among the thorns" on a planet which was far too humid, where the plant life was so powerful that it destroyed the equilibrium and the animal world. This world consisting only of plants still exists.

But the fourth attempt was finally successful on "good ground". And it is important to note that there were in fact three successes in all. This means that on two other planets, which are relatively near to you, there are living beings similar to yourselves who were created by the same creators.

"Hear, they who have ears". . . those who are able, understand. When the time comes, those who seek to understand will do so. The others, those who look without really seeing, and hear without really listening or understanding, such people will never understand the truth. On the other hand, those who prove their intelligence by their own efforts and thus show themselves to be worthy of their creators' help, they will be helped.

For the man who has, will be given more till he has enough and to spare; but the man who has not, will forfeit that which he has. *Matthew 13: 12*

The people who will not be able to prove their intelligence will not survive. Humans have almost proved that they are worthy of being recognised by their creators as their equals. They lack only . . . a little love. Love for each other, and particularly for their creators.

. . . It is given unto you to know the mysteries of the Kingdom of Heaven. *Matthew 13: 11.*

The three planets on which life has been created, have been set in competition against one another. The planet on which humanity makes the most scientific progress, thereby proving its intelligence, will receive the benefit of their creators' inheritance on the day of the "last judgement" – so long as they do not behave aggressively towards their creators.

This will be the day when their knowledge will have reached a sufficiently high level. At present human beings on Earth are not very far away from that day. Human genius is:

... the smallest of all the seeds, but when it grows up it is larger than any herb and becomes a tree, so that the birds of the air come and dwell in its branches. *Matthew 13: 32.*

The "birds of the air" here refers to the creators who will come and lodge in the branches; that is to say, will come to give their knowledge to humanity when humanity shows itself worthy of it.

The Kingdom of Heaven is like leaven which a woman took and buried in three measures of flour, until all of it was leavened. *Matthew 13: 33.*

This is another allusion to the three worlds in which the creators are waiting for science to bloom.

I will utter things hidden since the foundation of the world. *Matthew 13: 35.*

Here we have something fundamentally important. Planets have a life span, and one day they will no longer be habitable. By that time humanity must have reached a level of scientific knowledge sufficient either to undertake a move to another planet, or if it cannot adapt itself elsewhere, to create a humanoid form of life capable of surviving on another world. If the environment cannot be adapted to suit people, then people must be created who are compatible with the new environment.

For example, before humanity becomes extinct you would have to create another race of people capable of living in a totally different atmosphere who would inherit your knowledge before you disappear. So that this inheritance would not be lost, the creators put life on three worlds, and only the best one will be entitled to the inheritance.

So will it be at the end of the world: the angels will go out and separate the wicked from among the just. *Matthew 13: 49.*

The passage concerning the multiplication of bread has already been explained. It refers to concentrated food products in the form of large pills, rather like those containing all the vital elements, which your astronauts use. Your "Holy Bread" hosts are reminiscent of these pills. With the equivalent of a few loaves of bread, there is enough to feed thousands of people.'

Scientific Miracles

'WHEN Jesus walked on the water, the creators supported him using an anti-gravity beam which cancelled the effect of weight at a precise point.

He came to them walking upon the sea. *Matthew 14: 25.*

The beam, in fact, created a turbulence which is described as follows:

But seeing the wind strong, Peter was afraid . . . and when they got into the boat the wind fell. *Matthew 14: 30–32.*

The "wind ceased" as they boarded the boat, because the beam was switched off when Jesus reached it. Another totally scientific "miracle".

In reality there are no such things as miracles, only differences in levels of civilisation. If you had landed at the time of Jesus in a spacecraft, or even a simple helicopter, even though your level of scientific development may have been limited, you would in the eyes of the people of that time, have been performing miracles.

Just by producing artificial light, coming from the sky, driving a car, watching television, or even by killing a bird with a gun, because they would have been incapable of understanding the mechanism behind such phenomena, people of the time would have seen in them a divine or supernatural force. Also do not forget that the same scientific gap which exists between you and the people at the time of Jesus, also exists now between you and us. We can still do things which you would consider "miracles".

But for the most advanced individuals among you, they would no longer really be miracles since for the last few decades, you have taken the path of science and are trying to grasp the reason behind things instead of dumbly prostrating yourselves on your bellies and bringing offerings.

Our knowledge, however, remains such that if we decided to perform a few miracles, even your most eminent scientists would be unable to understand how we did them. There are some particularly well developed minds who would be able to cope with such things, but people in general would simply panic and we are still capable of astonishing people, even though they are no longer so easily shocked.

It is necessary for people to understand that there is no ethereal "God" but only people who created other people in their image.

In Chapter 17 of *St Matthew's Gospel* the creators appear once again.

Jesus took Peter, James and his brother John, and led them up a high mountain by themselves . . . and was transfigured before them. And his face shone as the sun, and his raiment was white as the light . . . and behold there appeared to them Moses and Elijah talking together with him . . . Behold, a voice out of the cloud said: this is my beloved son . . . hear him. *Matthew 17: 1–5*

This scene happens at night and the apostles are all frightened to see Jesus illuminated by the powerful searchlights of the spacecraft, out of which Moses and Elijah stepped, still alive thanks to the tree of life from which they had benefited. Immortality is a scientific reality, even if it does not correspond to humanity's idea of immortality. In Chapter 19 verse 30 of *St. Matthew* there is a sentence:

> But many who are first now will be last, and many who are last now will be first . . .

This means that the created shall become creators just as the creators were created.'

Deserving the Inheritance

'IN Chapter 25 of *St. Matthew's Gospel,* it is said that the three planets must make scientific progress and they will be judged one day. We read in the parable:

> For it is like a man going abroad, who called his servants and handed over his goods to them. . . And to one he gave five talents . . . to another, two . . . to another one. And he went on his journey . . . and he who had received five talents went back and traded with them, and gained five more . . . In like manner, he who received the two talents gained two more . . . but he who had received the one returned only one talent . . . Take away the talent from him, and give it to him who has ten talents. For to everyone who has shall be given, and he shall have abundance, but from him who does not have, even that which he seems to have shall be taken away. *Matthew 25: 14–29.*

Out of the three worlds where life has been created, the one which makes the most progress will receive the inheritance. The ones which have not progressed will be dominated by the other, and eliminated. This is also true on Earth between nations.

In *St Matthew's Gospel,* Chapter 26, Jesus reveals the importance of his death and of the writings which would later serve as proof. When one of his companions tried to defend him with a sword, he said:

> Put back your sword into its place . . . do you suppose that I cannot appeal to my father, who would at once send to my aid more than twelve legions

of angels?. . . How then could the scriptures be fulfilled which say that which must be? *Matthew 26: 52–54.*

It was in fact necessary for Jesus to die in order for the truth to be known throughout the world so that later on, when your creators return to Earth, they are not taken for usurpers or invaders. That is the purpose of the Biblical and Evangelical writings, to preserve traces of the work and presence of your creators, so that they will be recognised when they return.

After his death, Jesus was resuscitated with the help of the creators.

Suddenly there was a violent earthquake, for an angel of the Lord came down from heaven, and drawing near, rolled back the stone, and sat upon it . . . His face shone like lightning, his garments were white as snow. *Matthew 28: 2–3.*

The creators took care of Jesus and revive him. And he said:

Go therefore, and make disciples of all nations . . . teaching them to observe all that I have commanded you. *Matthew 28: 19–20.*

Jesus' mission was coming to an end:

So then the Lord, after he had spoken to them, was taken up into heaven. *Mark 16: 19.*

The creators took him away after this last most important phrase:

At the time of the end . . . if they shall take up serpents and if they drink any deadly thing, it shall not hurt them; and they shall lay hands upon the sick and they shall get well. *Mark 16: 18.*

This refers to humanity discovering anti-venom serums and antidotes, and developing surgery and so on – as is happening now.

In preparation for their arrival on Earth, the creators will appear more and more frequently, in order to give more weight to their revelations. This also is happening right now.

Look at the fig tree . . . when they put forth their buds, you know that summer is near. *Luke 21: 29–30.*

When unidentified flying objects begin appearing in large numbers, as they are doing at present, it means that the time has come. In the *Acts of the Apostles*, it says, furthermore, in Chapter 2:

And when the days of the Pentecost were drawing to a close, they were all together in one place . . . and suddenly there came a sound from heaven as of a violent wind blowing, and it filled the whole house where they were

sitting . . . and there appeared to them parted tongues as of fire, which settled upon each of them . . . they were all filled with the Holy Spirit and
began to speak in foreign tongues . . . *Acts 2: 1–4*.

To make it possible for the apostles to spread the truth throughout the
world, the creators exposed them to a concentrated burst of teaching, sent
to them by amplified telepathic waves, a little like electro-shocks, which
impregnated their memories with elements of other languages.

In the *Acts of the Apostles* note the numerous appearances made by the
creators – the "angels" – particularly when they liberated Peter, who had
been chained up by Herod:

And behold an Angel of the Lord stood beside him, and a light shone in
the room; and he struck Peter on the side and woke him, saying, Get up
quickly. The chains dropped and the angel said to him; Gird thyself and
put on thy sandals. And he did so. And he said to him, 'Wrap thy cloak
about thee and follow me . . .' And he followed him out, without knowing
that what was being done by the angel was real, for he thought he was
having a vision. *Acts 12 :7– 9.*

Peter, primitive as he was, thought he was having a vision as his chains
fell off. He did not know about the electric laser welding torch which was
being used by one of the creators. When such amazing things happen,
people think they are dreaming. This is why it was often said that people
who have seen the creators must have had a vision or seen them in a
dream. In the same way, it is said that people who have seen our flying
saucers must have had hallucinations. In that quotation it is clearly
explained that Peter thought he had seen everything in a dream but in fact
it was all very real.

And they came to the iron gate that leads into the city; and this opened to
them of its own accord . . . and straightway the angel left him. *Acts 12: 10.*

Another sign that the time has come is that the people of Israel have
regained their country.

And after these things I will return and will rebuild the tabernacle of
David which has fallen down. *Acts 15: 16.*

Another important sentence is found in *Acts 17: 29*, namely:

For we are also his offspring.

This was said by an apostle while speaking of "God".

We shall not continue to read further in the Gospels where there are many more references to the creators, because they are less important. You can interpret them yourself for those who ask questions in the light of the explanations I have already given you.'

And saying that, he left, just as on previous occasions.

5

THE END OF THE WORLD

1946, First Year of the New Era. The End of the Church.
The Creation of the State of Israel. The Mistakes of the Church.
The Root of all Religions. Mankind: A Disease of the Universe.
Evolution: A Myth.

1946, First Year of the New Era

THE next day, he returned just as before and started to speak.

'The time of the end of the world has arrived. Not the end of the world as in a catastrophe destroying the Earth, but the end of the world of the Church, which has completed its work. It performed this role more or less effectively. It was a task of vulgarisation making it possible for your creators to be recognised when they return. As you have noticed, the Christian church is dying. It is the end of this world because its mission has been fulfilled, albeit with quite a few mistakes because it tried for so long to deify the creators.

This deification was acceptable until the scientific age began. Then it should have been removed completely. This would have been possible had the truth been preserved or if people had been able to read between the lines. But too many mistakes were made.

This was foreseen by the creators, and the Church will collapse, because it is no longer of any use. In scientifically developed countries people are already consumed by a kind of moroseness because they have nothing left to believe in. Nobody can believe in a "Heavenly God" any longer, perched upon a cloud with a white beard, omniscient and omnipotent, which is what the Church wants us to do. Neither can anybody believe in delightful little guardian angels, nor in a devil with horns and hooves. So nobody knows what to believe in any more. Only a few young people have understood that love is essential. You have reached the golden age.

People of the Earth, you fly in the heavens and your voices are carried to the four corners of the Earth by means of radio waves. So the time has come for you to know the truth.

As it has been foretold, everything is happening now that the Earth has entered the Age of Aquarius. Certain people have already written about this, but no one believed them. Some 22,000 years ago your creators decided to start their work on Earth and everything that has happened since was anticipated because the movement of the galaxy implies this knowledge.

The Age of Pisces was the age of Christ and his fishermen, and the Age of Aquarius which follows began in 1946. This is the era in which the people of Israel found their country again:

And there shall be in that day, the noise of a cry from the Pisces Gate ... *Zephaniah 1: 10.*

The Gate of Pisces is the passageway into the Age of Aquarius. This is the moment when the Sun rises over the Earth on the day of the vernal equinox in the constellation of Aquarius. The loud clamour is the sound accompanying this revelation.

It is not by chance that you were born in 1946.'

The End of the Church

'THIS revelation, thanks to the enlightenment it contains, will bring new hope to people who are morose. But it will also hasten the fall of the Church – unless the Church can understand its mistakes and places itself at the service of the truth.

For the terrible one is brought to nought, and the scorner is consumed and all the watchers for iniquity are cut off. Those who by their word make man an offender, and lay a snare for him that reproveth in the gate, and turn aside the just for a thing of nought. *Isaiah 29: 20–21.*

It is the end of those people who want to make us believe in original sin

74

and who want to make us feel guilty; the end for people who lay traps for those who spread the truth at the end of the Age of Pisces and the beginning of the Age of Aquarius; the end of people who are trying to save the Church as it existed, while ousting the just, those who speak of justice and those who write or preach the truth. They are like the people who crucified Jesus. Such people were convinced that they were defending what was right without trying to understand and were frightened of being ruined and destroyed at the dawning of the Age of Pisces.

> The eyes of them that see shall not be dim and the ears of them that hear shall hearken diligently . . . the fool shall no more be called prince; neither shall the deceitful be called great . . . For the fool will speak foolish things, and his heart will work iniquity, to practise hypocrisy, and speak of Yahweh deceitfully, and to make empty the soul of the hungry, and take away drink from the thirsty . . . The villain's ways are villainous, and he devises infamous plans to ruin the poor with his lies, and deny justice to the needy. But the man of noble mind forms noble designs and stands firm in his nobility. *Isaiah 32: 3–8.*

Everyone in this case will understand the words: "the eyes of them that see shall not be dim". It is the Church who speaks of Yahweh deceitfully, and leaves empty the souls of those who are hungry for the truth.

It is the Church which devises infamous plans to ruin the poor so that those who are unable to understand, or who dare not understand, will remain faithful to it through the fear of sin, excommunication or other such nonsensical things. While the poor try to plead their case, those who lack the intelligence to seize the truth stand up for the lies of the Church at the Church's bidding. But those of noble mind, those who loudly proclaim the truth, they perform noble acts even though they may live without the approval of the organised Church.

> Do you not know, have you not heard, were you not told long ago, have you not perceived ever since the world began? Have you not understood from the foundations of the earth? *Isaiah 40: 21.*

> Here is my servant, whom I uphold, my chosen one in whom I delight; I have bestowed my spirit upon him, and he will make justice shine on the nations. *Isaiah 42: 1.*

You are the one who will spread the truth throughout the world, this truth which has been revealed to you over the past few days.

He will not break a bruised reed or snuff out a smouldering wick. *Isaiah 42: 3.*

You will not be able to destroy the Church and its lies completely, but eventually it will fade out by itself. This extinction has been going on for some time. The "wick" is weakening. It has accomplished its mission, and it is time for it to disappear. It has made mistakes and has enriched itself at the expense of the truth, without trying to interpret it in a clear enough way for people of this era. But do not be too hard on it, for it has spread throughout the world the word of the Bible which is a witness to the truth.

Its mistakes have been great, particularly when it injected too much of the supernatural into the truth, and wrongly translated the scriptures in ordinary Bibles. It replaced the term "Elohim" which refers to the creators, with a singular term "God", whereas in fact Elohim in Hebrew is the plural of Eloha.

In this way the Church transformed the creators into a single incomprehensible God. Another mistake was to make people adore a wooden cross in memory of Jesus Christ. A cross is not the Christ. A piece of wood in the shape of a cross means nothing:

> **Such a man will not use reason, he has neither the wit nor the sense to say: Half of it I have burnt, yes, and use its embers to bake bread; I have roasted meat on them too and eaten it; but the rest of it I turn into this abominable thing and so I am worshipping a log of wood.** *Isaiah 44: 19.*'

The Creation of the State of Israel

'THE return of the Jewish people to Israel, as it was predicted, is a sign of the golden age.

> **I will bring your children from the east and gather you all from the west. I will say to the north: give them up, and to the south: do not hold them back. Bring my sons and daughters from afar, bring them from the ends of the earth; bring everyone who is called by my name. All of whom I have created, whom I have formed, all of whom I have made for my glory.** *Isaiah 43: 5–7.*

This is indeed the creation of the state of Israel welcoming Jews from the north and from the south. The Bible, preserved by the Jewish people, bears witness to the coming of the creators as it is written in *Isaiah,* Chapter 43 verse 10: "You are my witnesses."

Lead out those who have eyes but are blind, who have ears but are deaf. Let all the nations be gathered together and the people assembled. Which of them proclaimed to us the former things and foretold this? Let them bring in their witnesses to prove that they were right, so that others may hear and say: it is true you are my witnesses, saith Yahweh, and my servant whom I have chosen: That you may know and believe me, and understand that I am he ... You are my witnesses, declares the Lord, that I am God, yes and from the ancient days I am one and the same. *Isaiah 43: 8–13*

"You are my witnesses." That is quite explicit, isn't it? And I can tell you again on this day – "from ancient days I am one, and the same" – thanks to the witness that you hold in your hand, the Bible.

For a small moment I have forsaken thee; but with great mercies I will gather thee. *Isaiah 54: 7.*

The Jewish people have, in fact, regained their country after having participated in safeguarding the truth.

The time when humanity will cure illness by scientific means is predicted:

There shall be no more thence an infant of days, nor an old man that hath not filled his days. *Isaiah 65: 20.*

Medicine helps people triumph over illness and especially over infant mortality.

In the lips of him that hath understanding, wisdom is found; but a rod is for the back of him that is void of heart. *Proverbs 10: 13.*'

The Mistakes of the Church

'THE Church was wrong in making human beings feel guilty and making them pray without seeking to understand. Because it is written in the Gospels:

When you pray, use not vain repetitions, as the heathens do: for they think that they shall be heard for their much speaking. *Matthew 6: 7.*

And despite the warning in the *Gospels,* the Church has also made itself too wealthy.

Lay not up for yourselves treasures on earth ... No man can serve two masters: for either he will hate the one, and love the other; or else he will hold to one, and despise the other. **You cannot serve God and Mammon.** *Matthew 6: 19–24.*

Elsewhere it says:

Provide neither gold, nor silver, nor brass in your purses, nor scrip for your journey, neither two coats, neither shoes, nor yet staves. *Matthew 10: 9–19.*

But with their stupid rules and meatless Fridays they were not obeying their own *Gospels*:

Not that which goeth into the mouth defileth a man; but that which cometh out of the mouth, this defileth a man. *Matthew 15: 11.*

How dare they, these men who are only men, indulge themselves in the wealth and luxury of the Vatican when the *Gospels* tell them to possess "neither gold, nor silver" – not even a spare coat?

How dare they preach goodness?

Then said Jesus unto his disciples, verily I say unto you, that a rich man shall hardly enter into the kingdom of heaven. *Matthew 19: 23.*

They make up heavy packs and pile them on men's shoulders; but they themselves will not move them with one of their fingers. But all their works they do for to be seen of men . . . and love the uppermost rooms at feasts . . . and greetings in the markets . . . For you have one master, and you are all brothers. Do not call any man on earth 'father', for you have one father, and he is in heaven. Nor must you be called 'teacher', you have one teacher, the Christ. But the greatest among you must be your servant. *Matthew 23: 4–11.*

That is all written in their own *Gospels.* So how dare the Church burden people with their so called sins, which are only different concepts of morality and lifestyles; how dare they speak of goodness while living in opulence in the Vatican when people are dying of hunger; how dare they seek invitations and honours while preaching humility; how dare they ask people to call them "Father", "Your Eminence", or "Your Holiness", when their Gospels expressly forbid all these things?

If tomorrow the Pope took to the road as a pauper, the Church would be revived – but it would have a totally different humanitarian goal to that which it has pursued up to now – namely the propagation of what must serve as proof for today.

That mission is finished but the Church could re-orientate itself towards goodness by helping those who are unhappy, by helping to spread the real truth of those writings, which until now, have been distorted or kept secret. In this way, the generous spirit of many priests would find fulfilment. For that to happen, the men of the Vatican should set an example by selling all their treasures to help finance underdeveloped countries. They should go to those countries and help people progress by offering practical help with their bare hands not just with "the good word".

It is unacceptable too that there are different categories of marriage and more particularly of burials, according to a person's wealth. This is another mistake of the Church.

But the time has come.'

At the Root of All Religions

'IT is not only in the Bible and the Gospels that there are traces of the truth; testimonies can be found in practically every religion. The Kabala especially is one of the richest in testimonies but it would not have been easy for you to get hold of one.

If one day you can find a copy, then you will be able to see that there are a great number of allusions to us. Particularly noteworthy is a description in the *Canticle of Canticles* (5) of the creators' planet and the distance which separates it from Earth.

It is written that the "height of the creator" is 236,000 "parasangs" and that "the height of his heels" is 30,000,000 "parasangs". The parasang is a unit of measurement just like the parsec which stands for the distance that light can travel in one second, which is about 300,000 kilometres. Our planet is 30,000,000 parasangs away from Earth or about nine thousand billion kilometres, just a little less than a light year.

By moving at the speed of light, or 300,000 kilometres per second, you would take almost one year to reach our planet. With your present day rockets which travel at only 40,000 kilometres per *hour,* it would take you about 26,000 years to reach our planet.

So you can see that we have nothing to fear for the time being. We have long since been able to travel to Earth from our planet in less than two months with an atom-based propulsion method which enables us to move at the speed of rays that are seven times faster than the speed of light.

Those rays "carry" us. To be carried by them, we leave the optical window, which is the spectrum of rays detected by the eye, to tune into the carrying beam. That is why people on Earth who have observed our spaceships have described them as becoming luminous, then very brilliant white, then blue, and finally disappearing. Obviously when a spacecraft goes beyond the speed of light, it disappears and is no longer visible to the naked eye. That is the "height of the creator's heels", the distance at which his heels, so to speak, rest on a planet.

The creators' own planet is 236,000 parasangs from its sun – a very big star – or seventy billion, eight hundred million kilometres. This is what is meant by the "height" of the creators.

The Kabala is the closest book to the truth but almost all religious books allude to us with varying degrees of clarity. This is especially true in those countries where the creators had their bases – in the Andes, in the Himalayas, in Greece where Greek mythology also contains important testimonies as well as in the Buddhist and Islamic religions and among the Mormons. It would take many pages to name all the religions and sects that testify in a more or less obscure way to our work.'

Mankind: A Disease of the Universe

'THERE, now you know the truth. You must write it down and make it known throughout the world. If people on Earth want us to give them the benefit of our experience and help them gain 25,000 years of scientific knowledge, they have to show us that they want to meet us and above all demonstrate that they deserve it so that all this can be done without any danger to us.

If we give our knowledge to humanity, we have to be sure they will make good use of it. Our observations in recent years have not shown that wisdom rules the Earth. Certainly there has been progress, but some people still die of hunger and a warlike spirit still exists throughout the world. We know that our arrival could improve many things and unite nations but we have to feel that people really want to see us and that they are truly ready to be unified.

We also have to feel that they really want to see us arrive, knowing fully who we are and understanding the true meaning of our arrival.

Several times human warplanes have tried to chase our craft, taking us for enemies.

You must tell them who we are so that we can show ourselves without any risk of either getting hurt or killed – which is not the case at present – or of creating a dangerous and murderous panic.

Some researchers want to contact us by radio. But we do not respond because in this way they could locate our planet. On the other hand, transmission times would be too long and our broadcasting system uses waves that your technology cannot pick up, because you have not yet discovered them. They are seven times faster than radio waves, and we are experimenting with new waves that are one and a half times faster than that.

Progress continues, and our own research continues for the purpose of understanding and relating to the large being of whom we are a part, and on whose atoms we are parasites. These atoms are the planets and the stars. In fact we have been able to discover intelligent living beings in the infinitely small, who live on particles that are planets and suns to them. They ask the same questions as ourselves.

Humanity is a disease inside this gigantic being and the planets and stars are its atoms. Also this same gigantic being is in its turn a parasite on other greater atoms. In both directions infinity exists. But the important thing is to make sure that the disease which is humanity continues to exist and never dies.

We did not know when we were creating you that we were accomplishing a secondary mission "written" into us, thus repeating what had been done for us.

From what we created and how it has developed we have discovered our own origins. For we were also created by other people who have since disappeared. Their world has quite certainly disintegrated, but thanks to them, we were able to continue in their steps and create you.

We may disappear one day, but by then you will have replaced us and taken over our roles. So you are the next link in the precious chain of human continuity. Other worlds exist and humanity is certainly developing in other parts of the universe.

But in this region of the universe, our world is the only one to have made new creations. This is important because each world needs to bring forth the innumerable children who are vital for preserving continuity. This allows us to hope that one day humanity will no longer be in danger of disappearing completely.

We are not sure that humankind can ever stabilise itself in abundance. The chain has always continued, but we must not upset the equilibrium of the immense body in which we are a parasite because we could trigger a catastrophe which at best might bring about a recession and at worst cause complete destruction.

In a healthy body a few germs can live without danger, but if they develop too much they cause a disease which troubles the organism. Then the organism reacts to destroy the germs responsible either naturally or with the help of medication. The important thing, apparently, is to create enough worlds so that humanity does not extinguish itself; then above all else to make sure that the equilibrium is not broken by concentrating our efforts anew on seeking to make those who exist happier.

It is in this area that we can help you tremendously.'

Evolution: A Myth

'FIRST of all you must dispel from your minds all uncertainty about evolution. Your scientists who have elaborated theories of evolution are not completely wrong in saying that humanity is descended from the monkey and the monkey from the fish and so on. In truth, the first living organism created on Earth was unicellular, which then gave rise to more complex life forms.

But this did not happen by chance! When we came to Earth to create life, we started by making very simple creations and then improved our techniques of environmental adaptation. This enabled us to make in turn fish, amphibians, mammals, birds, primates and finally man himself, who is just an improved model of the monkey to which we added what makes us essentially human.

In this way, we made human beings in our image, as it is written in the Bible in *Genesis*. You could have realised for yourselves that there is little chance of a series of accidents producing such a large variety of life forms – the colours of birds and their elaborate mating rituals, or the shape of certain antelope horns.

What natural need could lead antelopes or wild goats to develop curled

82

horns? Or birds to have blue or red feathers? And what about exotic fish? All that is the work of our artists. Do not forget the artists when you yourselves create life. Imagine a world without them – no music, films, paintings or sculptures . . . Life would be very boring and animals very ugly if their bodies corresponded only to their needs and functions.

Evolution of the various forms of life on Earth is really the evolution of techniques of creation and the increased sophistication of the creators' work. This eventually led them to create people similar to themselves. You can find the skulls of prehistoric men who were the first human prototypes. These were replaced each time by others more evolved. This continued right up to your present form, which is the exact replica of your creators who were afraid to create anything superior to themselves although some were tempted to do so.

If we could be sure that human beings would never turn against their creators to dominate or destroy them – as has happened between the different human races created successively on Earth – but instead would love them as parents, the temptation would be great to create an improved humankind.

This is possible but at what enormous risk! In fact some creators worry that the people of the Earth may be slightly superior to their parents. "Satan" is one of those who has always thought, and still does, that the people of the Earth are a danger to our planet because they are a little too intelligent. But the majority among us think that you will prove to us that you love us and that you will never try to destroy us. That is the least we expect before coming to help you.

It is even possible that at each creation of humankind by humankind, a small improvement is achieved, a true evolution of the human race which is gradual so that the creators do not feel threatened when faced with their creations.

This makes it possible to speed up progress. Although we do not think that at present we can give you our scientific heritage, we do feel it is safe to give you our political and humanitarian knowledge.

This will not threaten your planet, but will allow you to be happier on Earth. Thanks to this happiness you will progress faster and that could also help you to show us more speedily that you deserve our help and our inheritance in striving to achieve an intergalactic level of civilisation.

Otherwise. if humanity cannot calm its aggressiveness, if peace does not become your only goal, and you allow people to promote war, produce arms, test nuclear weapons, and maintain armies just to seize or retain power, then we will stop such people from becoming a danger to us, and there would be another Sodom and Gomorrah.

How could we not fear people from Earth when they attack their own kind – we who are from another world and slightly different?

You, Claude Vorilhon, you will spread the truth under your present name which you will replace progressively with RAËL. The literal meaning of "Raël" can also be simply translated as "messenger".

Furthermore it is through telepathy that we made you call your son Ramuel, which means "the son of the one who brings light", because he is truly the son of our messenger, of our ambassador.'

And following that pronouncement he left, just as he had done on other mornings.

6

THE NEW COMMANDMENTS

GENIOCRACY. HUMANITARIANISM. WORLD GOVERNMENT.
YOUR MISSION.

Geniocracy

I MET him the next day and again he began to speak.

'First of all, let us look at the political and economic aspects of life. What kind of people allow humanity to progress? The geniuses. Therefore your world must appreciate its geniuses and allow them to govern the Earth.

First of all, power was in the hands of brutes, who were superior to others because of their muscular strength. Next in power were the rich, who used their money to employ many 'brutes' in their service. Then came the politicians who ensnared the people of democratic countries with their own hopes – not to mention military men whose success has been based around the rational organisation of brutality.

The only type of people you have never placed in power are the ones who help humanity to progress. Whether they discovered the wheel, gun powder, the internal combustion engine or the atom, the geniuses have always allowed less intelligent people in power to benefit from their inventions. Often such people have used peaceful inventions for murderous ends. All that must be changed.

For this to happen, you must abolish all your electoral and polling systems because in their present form they are completely unsuited to human development. Each person is a useful cell in this huge body we call humanity. The cell in your foot should not decide whether or not your hand should pick up a given object. It is the brain which must decide, and if the object in question is good, the cell of your foot will benefit from it. It is not up to the foot to vote. Its job is simply to transport the body – including the brain – and it is not capable of judging if what the hand takes is good or not.

Votes only have a positive effect when there is an equivalence of knowledge and intellect. Copernicus was condemned by a majority of incompetent people because he was the only one at that time who had a sufficiently high level of comprehension. Although the Church – that is to say the majority – believed the Earth was the centre of the universe, this turned out to be wrong. The earth really revolved around the sun and Copernicus – the minority – turned out to be right.

When the first cars were invented, if we had asked everyone to vote to establish whether cars should be allowed to exist or not, the majority, who knew nothing about cars and did not care, would have responded negatively and you would still be riding in a horse and cart. So, how can you change all that?

These days, you have psychologists who are capable of creating tests to evaluate the intelligence and aptitude of every individual. These tests should be applied systematically from infancy onward in order to define each individual's orientation towards subjects studied.

When individuals reach a responsible age, their intellectual coefficient can be measured and included on their identity or voter's card. Only those with an intellectual capacity of at least fifty per cent above the average should be eligible for a public post. To vote, individuals would need an intellectual coefficient of at least ten per cent above average. If such a system existed now, many of your present politicians would not hold the positions they do today.

This is a totally democratic system. There are many engineers, for example, who are of lower than average intelligence, but who have very good memories and have obtained several academic degrees because of this.

On the other hand, there are many labourers or farm workers who have no specialised education at all, but whose intelligence is fifty per cent above the average. What is totally unacceptable now is that the voice of someone whom you might vulgarly call "a cretin" is worth as much as that of a genius who has thought maturely about the way he or she is going to vote. In some small cities elections are won by the candidate who buys people the most drinks – not by the individual whose policies are the most interesting.

Therefore right from the start, the right to vote should be reserved for those people whose brains are more suited to thinking and finding solutions to problems – that is to say an elite group of high intelligence. This does not necessarily mean those people who have done the most studying.

We are talking about placing the genius in power, and you may call that "geniocracy".'

Humanitarianism

'SECOND point: Your world is paralysed by profit, and Communism has failed to provide a carrot big enough to motivate people and encourage them to make progress.

You are all born equal and this is also written in the Bible. Your governments should ensure that people are born with approximately the same level of financial means. It is unacceptable that unintelligent children should live in luxury thanks to the fortunes amassed by their parents, while geniuses die of hunger and do any menial chore just to eat.

This way they forsake occupations where they could have made discoveries benefiting the whole of humanity. To avoid this, property ownership must be abolished without establishing Communism.

This world is not yours – that also is written in the Bible. You are only tenants. Thus all goods should be rented for forty-nine years. This will eliminate the injustice of inheritance. Your true inheritance, and that of your children, is the whole world if only you knew how to organise yourselves to make it pleasant. This political orientation of humanity is not communism; its preoccupation is the future of humanity. If you want to give it a name, call it "humanitarianism".

Take for example a man who has finished his studies at the age of twenty-one and wants to work. He chooses his profession and earns a salary. If he wants to find a place to live while his parents are still alive, he "buys" a house – but of course in reality he is renting a house or apartment for forty-nine years from the State which constructed it.

If the value of the house is estimated at 100,000 francs, he can pay that amount divided into monthly instalments for forty-nine years. At the age of seventy (twenty-one plus forty-nine) he will have paid for his house and can live there until his death, without ever paying again.

After his death, the house will go back to the State which must then allow his children, if there are any, to benefit from it freely. Supposing there is one child, then this child can live freely all his life in his father's house. At his death, his child in turn can also benefit from the family house and so on indefinitely. Inheritance must be completely abolished except for the family house. This does not, however, prevent each person being rewarded individually for their merits.

Let us take another example. Someone has two children. One is a good worker and the other is lazy. At the age of twenty-one they both decide to go their own separate ways. They each rent a house worth 100,000 francs.

The worker will rapidly earn more money than the lazy one. He will then be able to rent a house worth twice as much as the first one. If he has the means, he will even be able to rent both houses, one as a country house. If his savings are fruitful, he will also be able to build a house and rent it for forty-nine years, thereby receiving money due to him. But at his death, everything will go back to the community, except for the family home which will go to the children.

Thus individuals can make a fortune for themselves depending on their own merits, but not for their children. To each their own merits. The same should apply to commercial and industrial enterprises.

If someone creates a business, it is theirs for their entire life, and they can rent it out, but never for more than forty-nine years. The same goes for farmers. They can rent land and cultivate it for forty-nine years but after that it all goes back to the State which will be able to rent it out again for another forty-nine years. Their children can also rent it for forty-nine years.

This method must be adopted for all goods that remain exploitable, and as for the value of things, nothing changes. Everything that is of value such as shares, gold, enterprises, cash, or buildings are all owned by the community but may be rented for forty-nine years by those who have acquired the means by their own merits and labour.

In this way somebody who made a fortune around the age of forty will be able to construct houses, rent them as apartments for forty-nine years, and enjoy that money so long as life lasts.

Afterwards, the money which comes from these rents will go back to the community. This humanitarianism is already prescribed in the Bible:

> You shall count seven Sabbaths of years, that is seven times seven years, forty nine years. *Leviticus 25: 8.*

> When you sell or buy land amongst yourselves neither party shall drive a hard bargain. You shall pay your fellow countryman according to the number of years since the jubilee, and he shall sell to you according to the number of annual crops. The more years that there are to run, the higher the price, the fewer the years the lower the price, because he is selling you a series of crops. *Leviticus 25: 14–16.*

> No land shall be sold outright, because the land is mine, and you are coming into it as aliens and settlers. *Leviticus 25: 23.*

If geniuses are admitted to power they will understand the usefulness of these reforms. You must also see to it that all the nations of the Earth unite to form only one government.'

World Government

'THE creation of a new worldwide currency and a common language would help you to establish a world government. The Auvergne dialect is no longer spoken in Clermont-Ferrand, and very soon French will no longer be spoken in Paris, nor English in London, nor German in Frankfurt. Your scientists and linguists should unite and create a new language in all the schools of the world.

The same must be done with money. Worldwide currency values cannot be based on the franc, the dollar, or the yen, but must be based on a new currency created for the needs of the whole Earth so that people are not offended and forced to ask why another currency has been chosen instead of their own.

Finally the trigger required to bring about such a union is the suppression of military conscription, which teaches only aggressiveness to young men. Professional armies must then be assigned to protect public order. This must happen at the same time in all countries so as to provide an indispensable guarantee of security.'

Your Mission

'AS I have already told you, we know that our official arrival would accelerate many things. But we will wait until we see that human beings really want us to come, that they love us and respect us like the parents that we truly are – and that our spacecraft will not be threatened by your destructive military forces.

To achieve this, make it known throughout the world that you have met me and repeat what I have said to you. Wise people will listen to you. Many will take you for a madman or a visionary but I have already explained to you what to think of the foolish majority.

You know the truth, and we will stay in contact with you by telepathy to give you confidence and additional information if we think it is necessary. What we want is to see if there are enough wise people on Earth. If a sufficiently large number of people follow you, then we will come openly.

Where? At the place you will have prepared for our arrival.

Have a residence built in a pleasant country with a mild climate, with seven rooms always ready to receive guests, each with a separate bathroom, a conference room able to accommodate twenty-one people, a swimming pool and a dining room capable of seating twenty-one people.

This residence should be constructed in the middle of a park and should be protected from curious onlookers. The park should be entirely surrounded by walls to prevent anyone from seeing the residence and the swimming pool.

The residence should be situated at a distance of at least one thousand metres from the walls around the park. It will have a maximum of two stories and should be further screened from view by an inner barrier of trees and bushes. Install two entrances in the surrounding wall, one to the south and another on the northern side. The residence will also have two entrances.

There will be a terrace on the roof where a spacecraft of twelve metres in diameter may land. Access from that terrace to the interior is essential. The air-space above and around the residence should not be under direct military or radar surveillance.

You will try to ensure that the area where this residence is built – if possible larger than stipulated here – is treated as neutral territory by other nations and by the nation on whose territory it is located, by virtue of it being our embassy on Earth.

You may live with your wife and children in the residence which will be under your direction and you will be able to have servants there and invite guests of your choosing. However the area containing the seven rooms should be directly under the terrace and it should be separated from the section used by human beings by a thick metal door, lockable from the inside, which is kept permanently closed. An aseptic chamber should be built at the entrance to the conference room.

The financing of the project will be made possible through the help you receive from those people who believe in you, and therefore in us. They will be wise and intelligent and they will be rewarded when we come.

Keep a record, therefore, of those who contribute financially to the construction and upkeep of the residence, however modest their contribution. Also in each nation throughout the world appoint an individual who will be responsible for communicating these truths and who will help others join together to spread them.

Once a year, on a mountain near the residence, gather together from all over the world all those people who have heard about us and want us to come. Assemble the largest number of people possible, and have them think intensely about us and hope for our coming.

When there are enough people and when they wish intensely enough for us to come without any religious mysticism, but as responsible people respecting their creators, then we will land openly and give you our scientific knowledge as our heritage to all peoples of the Earth.

If those with warlike temperaments are rendered harmless all over the whole world, then this will happen. If the love of life and humanity's love for us and itself are strong enough, yes, we will come openly.

We will wait and see!

But if human beings remain aggressive and continue to progress in a manner which is dangerous for other worlds, then we will destroy this civilisation and its repositories of scientific wealth, and there will be another Sodom and Gomorrah until such time as humanity becomes morally worthy of its level of scientific understanding.

The future of humanity is in its own hands, and the truth is in yours. Communicate it throughout the world and do not be discouraged. We will never help you openly, or in any way that would give proof to the sceptics, since scepticism often goes hand in hand with aggressiveness. Intelligent people will believe you since what you will say contains nothing mystical. It is important to us that they believe you without any material proof. This proves to us more than anything else that they are intelligent and so are worthy to receive our scientific knowledge.

Now go. You will not be forgotten if you succeed during your life on Earth – or even after. If necessary we can wait until the time of your descendants to make our landing, because we can make you live again scientifically, just as we can resurrect all those who have led humanity along the path of human genius guided by the love of their creators – so long as their remains are preserved in coffins or tombs.

The only help we will give you will be to appear in the skies more and more frequently from now on in order to make people aware of the problems, and make them want to learn more about the truth that you are transmitting.

Gradually, thanks to these increased sightings, public awareness will also increase and our presence will no longer trigger stupid adoration, but instead a deep desire within the population to make contact with us.

You will call your movement Madech*– the "movement for welcoming the Elohim, creators of humanity", which carries in its initials a message, *Moise a devance Elie et le Christ* which means: Moses preceded Elijah and the Christ.

In French this is:

M: *mouvement pour* (movement for)
A: *l'accueil* (the welcoming)
D: *des* (of the)
E: *Elohim*
C: *createurs de* (creators of)
H: *l'humanite* (humanity)'

*Translator's note: In 1975, with the authorisation of the Elohim, the name of the movement was changed to the International Raëlian Movement.

7

THE ELOHIM

NUCLEAR WEAPONS. OVERPOPULATION. THE SECRET OF ETERNITY.
CHEMICAL EDUCATION.

Nuclear Weapons

'BEFORE we leave each other for the last time,' he said, 'do you have any questions to ask me?'

'You have interpreted the vision of Ezekiel as people equipped with space suits,' I replied, 'and you told me that the atmosphere of your planet was not the same as that on Earth. So why aren't you wearing a pressurised suit now?'

'Because we too have progressed scientifically and now we can do without them. My face seems to be in the open air but really it is protected by an invisible shield composed of repellent rays inside which I breathe different air from you. These rays let waves pass through, but not air molecules. It's a bit like the way you prevent fuel deposits escaping from certain ports in your technology by using emissions of bubbles.'

'Are nuclear weapons a danger for humanity?'

'Yes, a great danger. But if humanity does not become wise and peaceful, the existence of your nuclear weapons will mean that if the need arises, we will not have much to do in bringing about the destruction of your civilisation. Perhaps you might even destroy yourselves.

'If you do not, however, and if you become a threat to us, we will only have to destroy your stocks of bombs without sending offensive weapons against you. We could do this by rays, or even by telepathy, acting in such a way that in effect one of the great powers would become the aggressor and this would automatically release a fatal retaliation.

'If people do not want to be exposed to that danger any longer, all they have to do is take nuclear weapons away from the military. Such nuclear power used with care could enable countries which lack energy to make great strides forward. You urgently need to stop nuclear weapons testing, because you know nothing of the risks to which you are exposing yourselves. However, if humanity continues to play with nuclear weapons, it will simplify our task if we have to reduce you to silence.'

'Do you have any women on your planet?'

'Yes, it is mentioned in the Bible and I made you note the appropriate quotation.'

'And children also?'

'Yes, we can have children exactly like you.'

Overpopulation

'YOU told me you were immortal in some way. How do you prevent overpopulation?'

'This problem is in fact making itself evident very rapidly on Earth. To resolve it – and you should resolve it immediately because you are already sufficiently numerous – you must develop contraception and pass strict laws authorising women to have no more than two children.

'If two equals two, the population will arrive at a point where it no longer increases. We will be watching how well you deal with this too. It will be another test of your intelligence which will help us see if you have earned our heritage. This solution I offer is for humanity now where people only live for seventy-five years on average. For ourselves the problem is very different. We are not eternal but we are able to live ten times longer than you, thanks to a small surgical adjustment which in effect is the Biblical "tree of life". We have children, and we observe the rules which I have just explained: two parents, two children. This keeps our population constant.'

'How many of you are there?'

'We are a population of about seven billion.'

'We have met on six consecutive days, but did you always go back each time to your own planet?'

'No, I returned to an intergalactic ship which we use as a base and which stays constantly close to the Earth'.

'How many of you are on that vessel?'

'Seven, and on our planet there are seven provinces. Each has a representative on that vessel. If we add the two who are responsible for the vessel, there are permanently nine of us'.

'If the people here on Earth do exactly as you wish, what will happen?'

'We will come officially and land at the residence which you will have prepared. We will ask you to invite there the official representatives of the most important countries of humanity, in order to bring about total unification of the people on the Earth. If all goes well we will allow humanity to benefit step by step from our scientific advances. Depending on the uses that will be made of it, we will see if we can give humanity all our knowledge and allow you to enter the intergalactic era with our 25,000 years of scientific progress as your inheritance.'

'Are you the only world to have attained such an advanced level in science?'

'In this region of the universe, yes. There is an infinite number of worlds inhabited by beings of the humanoid type whose scientific level is lower than ours, although much superior to yours. What makes us fearful of disappearing is the fact that we have not yet found any planet with a civilisation as highly evolved as our own. We have economic relations with many other planets on which life has been created by other people who must have reached a scientific level equivalent to ours, because their religious writings prove this to us.

'Unfortunately, we have been unable to find the civilisations who created the closest of these worlds. But perhaps we will find them farther on as we continue to search the universe, each time moving further away. In most cases their planets approached the sun too closely and life became impossible, or their sun exploded, or became too cold. Although we have not noticed anything abnormal at present in our system, all this makes us fear the worst.'

'So there is no religion where you live?'

'Our only religion is human genius. We believe only in that, and we particularly love the memory of our own creators whom we never saw again and whose world we have never been able to find. They must have disappeared. However, they had taken the precaution of putting a huge space station in orbit around our planet, containing all their knowledge and this landed automatically when their world was destroyed. Thanks to them we have taken on the torch – and we would like to see this torch taken up by the people of the Earth.'

'And what would happen if your planet was destroyed?'

'In case our world is destroyed, the same arrangements have been made in advance so that you would automatically inherit all our knowledge.'

The Secret of Eternity

'DO you really live ten times longer than we do?' I asked.

'Our body lives on average, ten times longer than yours,' he replied. 'Like the first people of the Bible, that is between 750 and 1,200 years. But our mind, our true self, can be truly immortal. I have already explained to you that, starting with any cell of the body, we can re-create the whole person with new living matter. When we are in full possession of our faculties and our brain is at its maximum level of efficiency and knowledge, we surgically remove a tiny sample of the body which we then preserve. Then, when we really die, we take a cell from this preserved sample and re-create the body in full, just as it had been at the time the sample was taken.

'I say "as it had been at that time", meaning with all its scientific knowledge and, of course, its personality. But in this case, the body is made up of new elements with the potential for another one thousand years of life – and so on eternally. But in order to limit the growth of the population, only geniuses have the right to eternity.

'Everybody on our planet has a cell sample taken at a certain age, hoping that they will be chosen for re-creation after their death. In fact they not only hope for it, they try to earn this resurrection during their life. Once they have died, a grand council of the eternals assembles to decide in a "last judgement", who among those who died during the year deserves to live another life. For a period of three lifetimes, the eternal is on probation, and at the end of this time, the council of the eternals reconvenes to judge who, in the light of their work, deserves to join the council of the eternals as a perpetual member.

'From the moment that they wish to live again, they no longer have the right to have children, although this does not of course prevent love. This explains why the scientists who were members of the council of the eternals, wished to create life on other planets. They transferred their procreative instincts onto other planets.'

'What do you call yourselves?'

'If you wish to give us a name, even though we call ourselves men and women in our language, you may call us Elohim, since we did indeed come from the sky.'

'What language do you speak on your planet?'

'Our official language closely resembles ancient Hebrew'.

'Each day we have talked here, weren't you afraid other people might have surprised us?'

'An automatic system would have warned me immediately if people had approached within a dangerous radius, by air or by land'.

'What is your lifestyle and your work where you live?'

'Most of our work is intellectual as our level of scientific development allows us to use robots for everything. We work only when we feel the inclination – and then only with our brain. Only our artists and our sports people work with their bodies and only because they have chosen this.

'Our highly developed nuclear energy is almost inexhaustible, mainly because we have discovered a way to use the atom in a closed circuit. We also have many other sources of energy including solar energy and we do not necessarily use uranium in our nuclear reactors, employing instead many other simple and harmless materials.'

'But if you live so long, and do not work, do you not get bored?'

'No, never, because we always do things we enjoy doing – especially making love. We find our women very beautiful and we make the most of this.'

'Does marriage exist?'

'No. Men and women are both free. Couples exist. Those who have chosen to live as such may do so, but they may have their freedom whenever they wish. We all love one another. Jealousy does not exist, since everyone can have everything, and property is non-existent. There is no criminality where we live, thus no prisons and no police. However, there are many doctors, and regular medical visits for the mind.

'Those who show the slightest sign of psychological imbalance that could threaten the life or liberty of others, are immediately given treatment in order to bring them back to normal.'

'Can you describe the day of an average individual where you live?'

'In the morning they would get up and bathe, since there are swimming pools everywhere, have breakfast and then do whatever they feel like doing. Everybody "works", but only because they feel like working as there is no money where we live. Thus those who work always do it well, since it is by vocation.

'Only the eternals have specific tasks, for example supervising the electronic brains and computers used for dealing with vital functions such as energy, food and organisation. Of the seven billion inhabitants there are only 700 eternals and they live entirely apart from the others. They have the privilege of being eternals but with this goes the duty of doing everything for the others who are not obliged to work.

'To these 700 eternals we must add 210 probationers (about seventy each year, that is to say, ten from each province). Of the seven billion inhabitants, there are only about forty million children. It is only when they become of age – between eighteen and twenty-one years, depending on the individual – that the children undergo the operation which gives them a life span of more than 750 years. From then on, they too may have children. This enables the oldest of our non-eternal inhabitants to know their descendants for up to fifty generations.

'Out of seven billion inhabitants there are only about one million inactive people, and almost all of them are under treatment for psychological disorders. They are treated by our doctors for a period of six months. Most people are interested in arts, and they paint, sculpt, play music, write, produce films and participate in sports. We have a leisure civilisation in the full sense of the word.

'Our cities have an average population of about 500,000 people spread over a very small area. A city is in fact a huge house situated in a high place, inside which people can sleep, love, and do whatever they please. These city houses are about one kilometre in length and height and are traversed in all directions by waves used by everyone for travelling. You tie on a belt, and then place yourself in a wave current which transports you very rapidly to wherever you wish to go.

'The cities are tube-like in shape so that they do not eat up the countryside as they do where you live. Indeed one of your cities with say a population of about 500,000 covers a surface area twenty times greater than ours. The result is that when you want to go into the country, you have to travel for many hours, whereas in our case we are there in only ten seconds. An entire city is conceived by the same architect so that it will be pleasing to the eye and will harmonise perfectly with the scenery surrounding it.'

'But don't the people who have nothing to do get bored?'

'No, because we provide them with numerous activities. The individual's true value is recognised and everyone wants to show that they have worth. Whether it be in art, in science or in sports, each person wants to shine in order to become eternal, or simply to be admired by the community – or by a woman. Some people like to take risks and to deprive them of the risk of dying would take away their joy of living, and that is why dangerous sports are very popular.

'We can bring back to life any injured person but those who practise these sports may do so only if they state in writing that they agree not to be taken care of if they die during their sporting activities. We have a kind of atomic automobile race that would fascinate you and more violent activities like boxing, and even more violent than that, a kind of rugby game which is played in the nude, and where everything is permitted – boxing, wrestling and so on. All this may seem barbaric to you, but do not forget that all extremes must be balanced to avoid breakdowns.

'An extremely sophisticated civilisation must have primitive counterbalances. If our people did not have their idols in their favourite sport, they would have only one wish left, to die. The life of another individual must be respected, but their wish to die, or to play with death, must also be respected, and be permitted within well structured and well defined specialities.

'Where we live, contests are held each year in all branches of the various activities, one of which is a worldwide contest, permitting us to decide on the best individuals who deserve eternal life. Everyone lives only for that.

Each year, whether it be painting, literature, biology, medicine, or in any other speciality where the human brain can express itself, a competition takes place in every province.

'After a vote from the eternals of that province, "champions" are regrouped in the capital to submit themselves to the vote of a jury of eternals who designate those who become "champions among champions". These people are then presented to the council of eternals, who finally choose those who are worthy of becoming eternal probationers. This is the goal, and everybody's ideal. Distractions may well take on a primitive aspect when the supreme goal is so high.'

'Does this mean that the eternals have a totally different way of life from the other inhabitants?'

'Oh yes. They live apart in cities reserved for them and meet regularly to make decisions.'

'How old are the oldest ones?'

'The oldest, the president of the council of the eternals, is 25,000 years old, and you see him before you now. I have lived in twenty-five bodies up to this day, and I was the first one on whom this experiment was successfully carried out. That is why I am the president of the eternals. I myself directed the creation of life on Earth.'

'Then your knowledge must be immeasurable?'

'Yes, I have accumulated quite a lot of knowledge, and I will not be able to gain much more. It is in this way that the people on Earth may be superior to us because the capacity of that part of the brain which accumulates information, the memory, is larger. Human beings on Earth will be able to accumulate more knowledge than us, and therefore will advance further scientifically, if they have the means. This is what frightens those who oppose the council of eternals. People on Earth will be able to progress faster than us, if nothing stops them.'

Chemical Education

'THE knowledge that students need to accumulate must be enormous, and must take a very long time?'

'No. Thanks to an important scientific discovery, which in fact your scientists on Earth are beginning to consider, we can teach a student his lessons surgically. Your scientists have just discovered that if you inject the liquid from the memory of an educated rat into the brain of an uneducated rat, it will learn what the other knew.

'We can transmit information by the injection of brain memory matter, thus our children have almost no work to do. They regularly undergo injections of brain matter taken from people possessing the information necessary for instruction. Therefore, children only spend their time doing interesting things, which they decide on themselves, such as rebuilding the world in theory and fulfilling themselves in sport and the arts.'

'You never have wars among the provinces of your world?'

'Never. The sports competitions are sufficiently developed to eliminate the war instinct. Besides, psychologically, the fact that young people are able to risk their lives in games where systematically there are many deaths during each event, suppresses the war instinct.

This enables those who feel this instinct too intensely, to satiate it at the peril of their own life without involving those who do not want to travel along such perilous paths. If on Earth sports and games were more dangerous but organised, it would greatly reduce the chances of creating international conflicts.'

'Are the seven provinces of your world similar?'

'No, as on Earth there are different races and cultures. Our provinces were created and based on those races and cultures, while respecting the freedom and independence of each one.'

'Would it be possible for a man from Earth to visit your planet?'

'Yes, but you would have to wear a space suit adapted for your breathing. You could live without such a suit in a special residence where we have reproduced the Earth's atmosphere. There, many people from Earth live, including Moses, Elijah and Jesus Christ along with many other living testimonies of our creation. We will be able to bring all these people back to Earth when the time comes to support your statements.'

'Why not bring them back at once?'

'Because, in your incredulous world, if Jesus Christ returned, he would be placed in a psychiatric institution. Imagine someone landing among you saying he is the Christ. He would certainly be mocked and quickly locked up. If we intervened by performing scientific wonders to show he really was the Christ that would bring back religions based on God. It would also lend support to the idea of the supernatural or the mystical and we do not want either.'

Having said that, the small man saluted me for the last time, and told me that he would return only when all that he had asked of me was accomplished. Then he climbed back aboard his machine and it took off and disappeared just as it had on other mornings.

The Raëlian Movement

WHAT a story! What a revelation!

After returning home and classifying and copying up the notes I had taken, I realised the immensity of the task that had been entrusted to me.

I felt I had little chance of carrying it out. But since it is not necessary to hope in order to embark on an undertaking, I decided to do exactly what was asked of me, even though I might be taken for a visionary. After all, if being a visionary means having seen the light, then I am quite willing to be considered a visionary. It is better to be called a visionary and know the truth, than to be called clear-minded and not know the truth.

I wish to emphasise to sceptics of all kinds that I never drink alcohol and sleep very well at night. One can neither dream for six consecutive days, nor invent all this.

To you who refuse to believe me, I say: Watch the sky and you will see more and more sights that neither our scientists nor the military will be able to explain – except by foolish babblings aimed at saving reputations which they believe they would lose if the truth did not originate from someone in their closed circle. How could a scientist possibly not know? Those who condemned Copernicus – because he dared to say the Earth was not the centre of the universe – could never admit that someone other than themselves could reveal all that.

But all of you who have seen, or will see, unidentified flying objects which some people will explain away as dreams, or weather balloons, or even hallucinations, and all of you who dare not talk about it for fear of being mocked, it is only by getting together with those who believe, that you will be able to speak freely.

All these revelations brought me such a sense of well-being and such an inner peacefulness in this world where we do not know what to believe, where we cannot believe in a white bearded God or in a hoofed devil, and where official scientists cannot give precise explanations of our origins and our goals.

In the light of these amazing revelations, everything becomes so clear and is shown to be so simple. Knowing that somewhere in the universe, there is a planet full of people who created us to resemble themselves, who love us, all the while fearing that their creations might surpass them – is this not profoundly moving? Especially when we understand that soon it will be our privilege to participate in the further evolution of the humanity of which we are a part, by creating life ourselves on other worlds.

Now you have read this book that I have written, in which I have tried to set out as clearly as possible all that was said to me, if you simply think that I have a great imagination and that these writings were produced just to amuse you, then I will be profoundly disappointed.

But perhaps on the other hand these revelations will give you confidence in the future and allow you to understand the mystery of creation and the destiny of humanity. Perhaps they will answer the many questions that you have asked yourselves at night ever since your childhood, wondering why we exist and what is our purpose on this Earth.

If this happens I shall be very happy indeed.

Finally, if you understand that all I have said here is the profound truth and wish, as I do, to see these people land here officially very soon to give us their heritage and if you want to play a part in realising all that was asked of me, then I will have fulfilled my mission in writing this book.

If this is the case, write to me and we will welcome you into the Raëlian Movement. We will build the embassy they want and, when we are numerous enough internationally to welcome them with the respect and love that those who created us richly deserve, then they will land openly and we will become the beneficiaries of their immense knowledge.

To all of you who believe in God or in Jesus Christ, I say you were right in such a belief. Even if you thought all was not exactly as the Church would have you believe, there was a foundation of truth. You were right to believe in the basis of the scriptures, but wrong to sustain the Church. If you continue to distribute your money to provide cardinals with the finest vestments and, at your expense, continue to authorise the existence of the military and their nuclear threat, then it means that you wish to remain primitive and are not interested in entering the golden age to which we are now entitled.

If, however, you wish to participate passively or actively, according to your means, in the creation and development of the Raëlian Movement, take your pen and write to me. We will very soon be numerous enough to choose a piece of land on which the embassy will be built. If you still have doubts, read the papers and look at the sky. You will see that sightings of mysterious craft are becoming more and more numerous and this will give you the courage to send your letter to me, addressed to: Raël, c/o International Raëlian Movement. C.P. 225, CH 1211 Geneva 8, Switzerland.

2. Rael in 1996 - telling his story to television viewers from the pits at the Daytona 24-hour race in the United States.

1. Rael photographed in the mid-Seventies at the site of the first encounter on the Puy-de-Lassolas volcano, near Clermont-Ferrand, dressed in the clothes he was wearing on 13th December 1973.

3...and in another event at the wheel of his eye-catching racing car with its UFO and symbol of infinity logo.

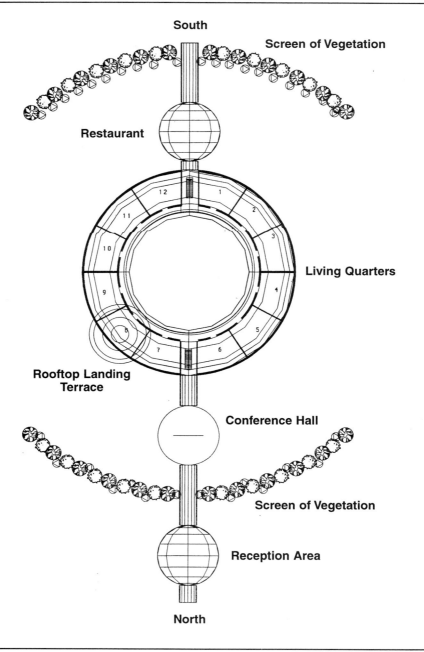

South

Screen of Vegetation

Restaurant

Living Quarters

Rooftop Landing
Terrace

Conference Hall

Screen of Vegetation

Reception Area

North

4. An architect's drawing of the planned extra-terrestrial embassy, based on details given to Rael during the second encounter of 7 October 1975.

5. A scale model of the embassy with an extra-terrestrial spacecraft on its rooftop landing pad.

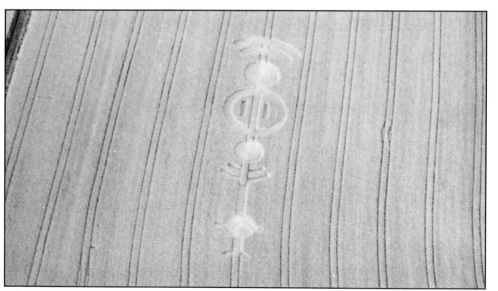

6. 'Some crop circles', says Rael, 'are made by the Elohim to encourage humanity to build the embassy'. This one, which appeared at Cheesefoot Head, Wiltshire in England in August 1990 bears a very close resemblance to the detailed plan of the building.

7. The symbol of infinity which Rael saw emblazoned on the UFO in 1973 is formed by interlocked Star of David triangles and a swastika which means 'that which is above is like that which is below and everything is cyclic'. The original emblem of the Raelian Movement, still used in Africa and Asia, it is seen here hand-painted on a whitewashed wall in French-speaking Africa. 'UFOs, The Truth Revealed At Last,' says the poster.

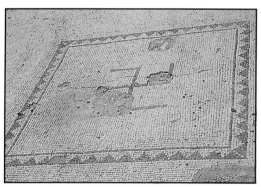

8. The Elohim's symbol is the oldest on Earth and its central swastika, meaning 'well-being' in Sanskrit, also represents infinty in time. Many traces of it were found in the ancient world and this mosaic was photographed inside a 3,500 year-old Israeli synagogue at Ein Gedhi close to the Dead Sea.

9. The complete original symbol is to be found on the Tibetan *Book of the Dead* or *Bardo Thodol.*

10. A medallion showing the revised Raelian symbol In 1991, out of respect for victims of the holocaust and in an effort to help the negotiations with the Israeli goverment concerning the building of the extra-terrestrial embassy, Rael changed the symbol of the Movement for western countries, replacing the swastika with a galaxy-shaped swirl which also represents infinity in time.

BOOK TWO

EXTRA-TERRESTRIALS
TOOK ME
TO THEIR PLANET

INTRODUCTION

WHEN I started this second book I wanted simply to relate what my life had been like before my fantastic encounter of 13 December 1973. That was necessary to answer the many people who had asked firstly what I had done before that time, and secondly whether anything extraordinary had happened to me during my childhood that could have foreshadowed such a destiny.

I was surprised myself as I searched my memories, for even though I thought that nothing extraordinary had occurred at the beginning of my life, I found scenes resurfacing which formed a whole when put together, and I saw that my life had really been guided for me to be what I was, and to find myself where I did, on December 13, 1973.

I had almost finished writing this account when the second encounter took place. Consequently, I have summed up my early memories briefly in order to give as much space as possible to the second part of this message and to provide a full account of this second contact, which turned out to be even more fantastic than the first.

1

MY LIFE UNTIL THE
FIRST ENCOUNTER

Two Years Have Passed

TWO years! For almost two years now I have been trying somehow to radiate this truth which often seems too great for me. Time goes by, and I feel I am getting nowhere. Yet little by little a solid core of people is forming around me, people who understand that *The Book Which Tells the Truth* really does just that.

There are seven hundred of them as I pen these lines, and I understand how this is both few and many at the same time. Few when we consider the four billion people who populate the Earth, and many, when we consider how few people had decided, after two years, to follow the man who, two thousand years ago, had the equally heavy burden of being initiated and then initiating the primitive people of his time.

Who are these seven hundred? Are they, as the scoffers would no doubt love to believe, average simpletons who could be made to swallow anything? Not at all. Some of them are university graduates or people holding PhDs in philosophy, psychology, theology, sociology, medicine, physics and chemistry.

My admiration perhaps goes as much to those who have no degree, since although they have not acquired knowledge through studying that would allow them to realise that living matter and people like us can be created scientifically, they are still able to feel it intuitively, as people capable of mastering matter and putting themselves in harmony with the universe of which they are a part.

I must say that I am optimistic on the whole, and that I believe that I have so far led the mission that has been entrusted to me along the right path. For whatever happens to me, *MADECH is up and running and nothing will ever be able to stop it.

In two years I have given nearly forty lectures, and since certain questions come up regularly, I suppose some parts of the message need to be clarified. So I will try to do that in this work.

First of all, what sort of life was I leading before the encounter of 13 December 1973?

I have to admit I have only recently begun to look back on my life to figure out exactly how it had been guided for me to be available and ready to go into action on the spiritual, psychic and emotional levels at that time. Certain events in my childhood had never seemed to me to have the least meaning when taken separately – but they did when taken together.

Now it all seems very clear to me, and I am moved when I remember some things that I considered unimportant at the time they occurred. Far be it from me to tell my life story in a way that suggests that each event in it was exceptional, but it seems that many people want to know more about what had happened to me before. Also, rather than leave it to wagging tongues, I would rather tell it all myself.

Childhood: a UFO over Ambert

AS the child of an unknown father, I cannot say that I had a typical childhood. I was what is called a 'natural' child – as if all others were 'artificial' children.

My birth was an accident as it were – at least for the little town of Ambert which is so devoutly Catholic that it is known as the 'world capital of the rosary'. Furthermore the unknown father, who was not totally unknown, was apparently, a Jewish refugee. What sacrilege!

My birth was concealed as much as possible – not in a cave, but in a clinic at nearby Vichy. It occurred on 30 September 1946 at about two o'clock in the morning, and was a very difficult one. But the important thing is that I was conceived on 25 December 1945. Conception, the moment when a being truly begins to exist and develop in the womb of its mother, is the true date of birth for each individual. December 25 has been

* Now renamed the International Raëlian Movement – see footnote, page 92

a very important date for almost two thousand years now. For those who believe in coincidences, my life began with a coincidence.

When we returned to Ambert, my poor mother tried for a long while to pass me off as 'the son of a friend she was taking care of for a while.' We lived under the same roof as her father who, if he held it against her when he learned the truth, proved to be the nicest of grandfathers to me during the short time I knew him. Sadly, he died when I was still a very young child. I was later told about how amused he looked when, having seen him trim his fruit trees, I took a pair of scissors to cut . . . his lettuce.

I was raised by my grandmother and my aunt who were then, and still are, living together. They taught me to read and helped me take my first steps, which I remember very clearly – surely the earliest memory of my life.

It was only very recently that my grandmother told me that in 1947 she saw a strange craft flying very quickly and noiselessly over Ambert near her house. She had never dared tell anyone about it for fear of being accused of hallucinating. It was only after reading my book that she decided to talk to me about it . . . and at the same time she decided to join MADECH. Her decision to join was, in fact, one of the most important forms of encouragement that I received.

The Pope of the Druids

IN Ambert there was an old man of whom small children were afraid, and of whom the grown-ups made fun. They nicknamed him 'Jesus Christ' because he had very long hair rolled up in a bun, and a magnificent beard. He was always clad in a long cape that came down to his ankles, and he lived about a hundred metres from the house where my mother had found a small apartment. He did not work and nobody knew how he could afford to live in the minuscule house in front of the municipal grammar school.

As they got older, the children lost their fear of him, and, like their parents, started to make fun of him, laughing and making faces as they followed at his heels.

Personally, I did not enjoy playing with the others, preferring to contemplate insects and look at books. I had passed this man in the street several times and had been surprised by his face, which radiated great kindness, and by the mischievous smile he wore whenever he looked at me. I did not know why, but he did not scare me, and I did not see anything laughable about him. Also I did not understand why the other children made fun of him.

One afternoon I followed him, curious about where he was going, and saw him go into his house, leaving open the door that led into a small, very dark kitchen. I went closer and could see him sitting on a stool with the mischievous smile on his face, as if he were expecting me. He motioned for me to come nearer. I went inside the house and moved towards him.

He laid his hand on my head and I felt a strange sensation. At the same time he looked up in the air and uttered some words that I did not understand. After a few minutes had passed he let me go, still without saying a word, and still smiling the same mysterious smile.

All this had me puzzled at the time, but I very quickly forgot about it. It was only in the summer of 1974, when reading a book that my mother had lent me about the mysteries of Auvergne, that I learned that Father Dissard, the old man in question, was the last Dissard – that is, the last living 'Pope' of the Druids – and that he had been dead for several years.

Then I recalled the scene from my childhood, and thought again of the mysterious smile that the old man used to give me each time I passed him in the street – which was every day, since we had been virtually neighbours. I now know exactly who he was addressing when he looked up in the air and uttered those mysterious phrases, just as I know exactly what the silent, luminous machine was that my grandmother had seen.

One other thing also comes to mind again. After the scene that took place at Father Dissard's house, I went to sleep every evening counting up to nine a certain number of times.

This is a number that has frequently come up in my life, like a code that has been assigned to me. I have never been able to explain this sudden habit, which began several years after I had learned to count much higher than nine, and therefore could not have been the result of learning by rote. I was seven years old when this incident took place.

Poetry

AT that time what mattered most to me were animals, which I loved to draw all day long, when I was not organising snail races. I was fascinated by animal life and I dreamt then only of becoming an explorer, so as to be able to get near the mysterious fauna of the virgin forests.

But at nine years of age – the number nine again – everything was to change. First of all I was discovering what was to become a true passion for me – speed. Speed that is, on everything with wheels, with or without an engine. Speed and especially balance, the feeling of motion and the struggle against oneself, against one's own reflexes. In fact the ultimate mastery of mind over body.

It started with wild downhill runs on a little bicycle with almost no brakes, and I wonder how it was that I did not fall a single time. To liven things up, I would position myself at the top of a hill and wait for a fast car to pass by. Then I would launch into dizzying pursuit, catch up with the car and pass it – to the driver's great surprise – and, once at the bottom of the hill, I would turn and go back to wait at the top for another car.

A few months later, I found myself by chance attending the Tour de France motor race and it was love at first sight. It was possible, I then realised, to know the joys of high speed without having to pedal back up a hill. And you could make it your job.

I made up my mind, the way you can when you are nine years old. I would be a racing driver.

From that day on my life was centred only around motor racing. Nothing else interested me and I did not see the point of learning all they taught me at school, since I was going to be a racing driver. Children's comics were replaced by serious motor magazines, and I impatiently began counting off the years that separated me from the age when I could obtain a driving licence.

It was also at the age of nine that I had my first experience of boarding school. My mother was in despair because I no longer wanted to do anything at school and I constantly told her that such learning was useless for motor racing drivers. So she decided to send me to the Notre-Dame-de-France boarding school in Puy-en-Velay.

She hoped that without motor racing magazines I would apply myself to school work, and in a way she was not far wrong. But I have very bad memories of that first boarding school, almost certainly because I was too young when I was sent there.

I remember that I spent many nights crying in a huge dormitory, where what I now believe I missed most was the chance to be alone and meditate. This need, which caused me to spend entire nights crying, further increased my already great sensitivity, as will any emotional need that is denied. Then I discovered poetry.

I had always been more attracted to literature than to mathematics, although only as an interested and passive reader. Then came the desire, the need to write – in verse if possible. I remained uninterested in mathematics yet I had now achieved a solid average in that subject as in all others. But in French language, and especially writing, I regularly came first – as long as I liked the set subject. I even wrote an entire collection of poems and won first prize in a poetry competition.

The most surprising thing was that even though I had not been baptised, I was in a private boarding school run by Catholic monks, with all the praying which that involves – prayers before eating, and going to bed, before rising in the morning, before studying – and attending daily mass with communion. When, after six months of daily communion, the brethren discovered that I had not been baptised, they seemed utterly horrified. I actually thought it was funny; it was in fact the only part of their mass that I liked, this free tasting of morsels of bread.

It was also at the age of nine that I attained puberty. I enjoyed it very much and discovering unknown and secret pleasures which no other nine year-old in the dormitory seemed yet to know about was some consolation for my incomplete solitude.

Finally, it was at the age of nine that I fell in love for the first time – and it was the intense kind of love that can seize children at that age. Due to my improved classroom results, my mother had agreed not to send me back to boarding school, and I found myself in the fourth grade at the municipal grammar school in Ambert. There she was, nine years old or almost, and her name was Brigitte. I was shy and blushed quite ridiculously. It took only a glance during a medical visit, or perhaps a gesture of modesty to hide a non-existent bosom from my eyes, to release in me feelings of tenderness and a great desire to protect this so evidently fragile being.

The following year I found myself at the same school, in the fifth grade, in the company of my first love to whom I dared not even speak. Still, I managed to end up sitting one desk in front of her at the beginning of the school year so that I could turn my head from time to time and admire her beloved face. I was only ten and was always thinking about her.

The fact that I was close to her in class spurred me on and I set myself to work hard enough to avoid having to repeat a year. In this way I moved up to the sixth grade without the least interest in my studies.

Unfortunately we were now constantly changing classes and had different teachers instead of just one. As a result, I was almost always separated from her, and did practically no work – so much so that the next year I found myself back in a boarding school in the small village of Cunlhat, which is about thirty kilometres from Ambert.

It was even worse there than it had been at Puy-en-Velay. We were all crammed into a tiny dormitory that was barely heated and, worst of all, there was virtually no discipline. So the biggest and strongest boys enforced their own law. I think that is where I developed such a hatred of violence.

One day, fed up with being bullied by boys against whom no disciplinary measures were ever taken, I took to the road on foot, determined to cover the thirty kilometres that separated me from my maternal home. Nobody noticed my departure, and when the school principal caught up with me in his car, I had already walked nearly ten kilometres.

To my great delight I was kicked out of the school, and sent back to the Catholic brethren at Ambert in the middle of the school year as a day boy. What joy! I could now see Brigitte every day in the street. By then she was twelve, her small bosom was budding deliciously, and to me she was more beautiful than ever.

I grew less and less interested in my studies and began to taste the joys of playing truant, mainly because I did not like finding myself back among the priests, who had quickly advised my mother to have me baptised. Fortunately, she preferred to wait until I was old enough to understand, so that she could ask my opinion.

What I would have liked at that time was to become a garage mechanic, because I had learned that that this was a useful skill for racing drivers. My mother, who hoped I would become an engineer, wanted me at all costs to continue with my studies so she would not allow me to become apprenticed to a garage.

Renewed experience of bullying gave me the desire to write poems again, and I started pacing about in the country with a notebook in my hand instead of attending classes.

At fourteen I found myself back in boarding school once more, this time in Mont-Dore, at a grammar school where they take children not wanted by any of the other schools in the region.

· I found myself in the company of a fairly interesting collection of dunces and 'hard cases'. It was one of the latter, a typical boarding school 'big shot', who ended up being responsible for the direction I took during the next ten years of my life. His name was Jacques and he played the electric guitar, which quite impressed me. As soon as the Christmas holidays came, I got my grandmother to buy me a magnificent guitar, and Jacques taught me a few chords. Then I started setting my poems to music, and noticed that it was apparently very pleasing to those who listened. As soon as the summer holidays came, I began to enter some radio singing contests, which I almost always won.

It was also during that summer vacation that I discovered physical love for the first time – with a barmaid who had been enchanted by my songs. She was twenty years old and did not teach me much apart from the effects that the guitar can have on women.

The following year I was fifteen, and wanted more than ever to live my own life. One day I took my guitar under my arm along with a small suitcase, said farewell to the boarding school with its uninteresting studies, and hitch-hiked to Paris. I had two thousand old francs in my pocket and a heart full of hope. At last I was going to earn my own living, save up enough money to take my driving test at the age of eighteen and become a racing driver.

By a stroke of luck I was picked up by a man driving a car that had tremendous acceleration hidden beneath discreet-looking bodywork. When he told me he was a racing driver and gave me his name, I was able to tell him which car he had driven and the awards he had won. He was flattered and surprised, little-known as he was, to meet a young boy who remembered all his achievements. He told me that he had once been a clown, and that he now owned a garage in the south-west. When we arrived in Paris he invited me out to dinner, and even offered me a room in the hotel where he was staying.

In the lounge we chatted a bit with two young women who were dance hostesses in a bar and had finished their day's work. I sang some songs and then we went to bed, each with one of our charming companions. There I was truly initiated into physical love making.

The next morning I left discreetly, because I wanted to find a room and some cabarets that would be interested in my songs. I did not find either and spent my second night in Paris in the subway with the tramps.

I had not a penny left and the next morning I was starving. I spent my day dawdling and despairing of ever sorting anything out. But that evening I saw a man playing an accordion on a café terrace and the customers were throwing him coins. I decided to try the same thing and right from the start it worked very well. I was saved.

I lived like that for three years, often sleeping anywhere and eating a sandwich from time to time. But I made enormous progress, and one day I was hired by a small cabaret on the Left Bank. I made ten francs each night and needed fifteen for the taxi ride back to Montmartre where I lived in a small room. Yet I had my name on the poster – although in small print! Already I was imagining my name high up on the poster in big letters, seeing the success I was having every night.

One day I met the actor Jean-Pierre Darras, who advised me to take acting classes to improve my stage presence. Since I did not have the means to pay for them, he kindly arranged for me to attend a course at the National Theatre of Paris free of charge. So for three months I took the Dullin course – and then gave it up because I did not feel at all attracted to the theatre.

I used to introduce myself at the time under the pseudonym of Claude Celler, which I had chosen as a tribute to the skier and champion racing driver, Tony Sailer. I modified the spelling so that my initials would become C C – retaining my real first name.

I began to win a lot of radio contests and, by singing in several cabarets, I was able to live reasonably well, and more importantly to save up enough money to take my driving test at exactly eighteen, as planned.

But that was not enough to become a racing driver. First I had to make a name for myself in the hope of being hired by a major company, and for that I needed to have a competition car, participate in some races independently and, if possible, win them. A racing car is very expensive, and I had to continue saving in the hope of acquiring such a vehicle. I continued with my singing, and tried to put some money aside. Many writer-composer friends had made recordings and seemed to be making a lot of money from them. So I decided to try it, having by now more than 150 songs in my bag.

The first recording firm that I approached offered me a three-year contract, which I signed. The director of the recording firm was Lucien Morisse, the director of the radio station Europe No. 1, which had launched a tremendous number of famous singers. My first record was fairly successful, and the second, thanks to a song called *Le Miel et la Canelle* (*Honey and Cinnamon*) – was even more popular. It was often heard on the radio:

HONEY AND CINNAMON

I smell honey and cinnamon
I smell vanilla and love
I smell honey and cinnamon
Girls I'll always adore.

The first was a brunette, Margot was her name
We played the pipes as the moon lit the night
I took the road to her eyes
And followed the way to her hair.

The second was a blonde, her name was Marielle
The path around her curves I remember well
I took the road to her eyes
And followed the way to her hair.

The third was a redhead, Marion she was called
For her lovely little face and her frothy underslip
I took the road to her eyes
And followed the way to her hair.

Don't cry, my friend, for tomorrow will be spring
They are so lovely and you're not twenty yet
I took the road to her eyes
And you can travel the path to her hair.

I was giving many performances and taking part in many road shows. Everything was going well and I even had the pleasure of being selected to participate in the Golden Rose song contest held in Antibes.

But those who were guiding me did not really want me to become too famous an artist. That stage of my life had been planned to develop my sensitivity, and to accustom me to expressing myself in public, but no more than that.

Even though the fact that I was among the contestants selected for the Golden Rose was being announced on the radio every morning, Lucien Morisse came to me one day and explained that he had to withdraw me from the contest. He said that I would understand why later, but he could not tell me more at that moment.

So in the end I did not participate in that Golden Rose contest but had to continue to live on what I could earn from my singing which, I realised, would never be enough to buy a car that would get me into racing. Therefore, when I was offered the opportunity to become a representative for the company where I did my recording, I accepted immediately, convinced that I would be able to save up enough for a car in a few months.

I found myself back in Bordeaux, where I was a commercial agent in charge of fifteen regions. I stayed there for a year and left when at last I had enough money to buy myself a competition car. I just had time to break that car in before a friend wrote it off in an accident. However I had composed new songs during the year in Bordeaux and a wealthy friend urged me to make another record, which he would finance himself.

I spent another year living on my poetry and then, as if to make me change my lifestyle radically, I was involved in a very serious car accident.

On a very tiring tour I fell asleep at the wheel of my car and struck a wall head on, at about 100km per hour – 60 mph. More than ten people had already died at that spot. I came out of it with several fractures, but alive. I was immobilised for three months or more and my savings ran out. I was still not racing. I, who had dreamt of starting out at eighteen, had still not entered a single race by the age of twenty-two.

Having been to racing circuits many times as a spectator, I had noticed how infatuated young people were with this sport, and also the number of boys who wanted to be racing drivers without knowing how to proceed. I did not know much more than they did, and told myself that the best way for me to enter the racing scene would be to find a career that took advantage of their enthusiasm. I knew how to write, so the solution was obvious. I would become a reporter for a sports car magazine.

I got in touch with a number of specialist magazines, but in vain because so many other enthusiasts had come up with the same idea. Then I noticed a small advertisement in the motor section of *L'Equipe* from someone looking for photographer-reporters, no experience required.

I wrote, and the advertiser replied saying that my application was being considered, but that I had to send 150 francs for administrative costs. In exchange, I would receive some film to make a test report on a subject of my choice. I sent the money, got back the film and wrote the report – on a motor race, of course – and immediately sent it to the address indicated.

Very soon afterwards, I received a letter asking me to call a number in Dijon, where the head office of the firm that had placed the advertisement was situated. I met the head of the publishing company – a man of about thirty years of age who claimed to have made a fortune in photography in the United States.

He seemed to be very interested in my ideas about the creation of a sports car magazine intended for young people who hoped to become racing drivers and offered to hire me as editor-in-chief of a newspaper that was to come out in a few months' time. He showed me the factory that he was going to buy to set up his printing office, introduced me to the printer in Dijon whom he had hired to be the director, and showed me the house where my wife and I could live, at a stone's throw from my office.

I replied that it would suit me provided I could cover and participate in races. He then told me that he was also looking for someone capable of running a competitions department, since he intended to launch the new newspaper by racing some cars painted in his own colours. That would enable me to be right where the action was, and I agreed to be the director of the competitions department for this company.

A week later, I moved from Paris to Dijon with my wife, Marie-Paul. I had been married for about three months, and she was expecting our daughter. I had met Marie-Paul in the month of June, and we had not left each other's side since the first day we met. We had married three months later, only because her family was shocked to learn that we had no intention of getting married religiously. Her family was very old-fashioned and at first I prayed with them before meals.

My stay in Dijon, however, lasted only two months and I received no salary. It transpired that the 'rich American' who had wanted to create a newspaper had in fact just come out of prison without a penny. He had swindled sums of money ranging from 150 francs to 300 francs from more than 500 young people dreaming, like me, of becoming racing drivers or photographer-reporters.

I had worked two months for nothing, and I found myself full of ideas, but penniless. This time I decided to make a start alone in the great world of publishing. I moved to Clermont-Ferrand, close to my mother who was then looking forward to becoming a grandparent very soon, and started my own publishing house to produce a magazine in my own way. Copies of that magazine were soon on sale, thanks to a printer who also loved sports cars, and who agreed to take the risk of extending me credit, although I could not give him any form of guarantee.

The magazine took off quickly and soon became one of the leaders in its field. I reserved for myself the most interesting task – test driving new models on the magnificent circuit of Mas-du-Clos, at Creuse, and on the road. By this means I gained entry into the world of motor sport and cars were lent to me to race. At last my dream was becoming a reality and, what is more, I found from the start that I was a gifted competition driver, gaining many victories with cars that were unfamiliar to me.

For three marvellous years I lived like this, all the time making continuous progress with my driving technique, and concentrating 100 per cent on the field that I loved – that of sports cars. I must say that I felt a real pleasure in steadily pushing back my limitations and constantly improving control of my reflexes and reactions. However, I did not care for either engine noise or the smell of burning fuel and I dreamed of days to come when racing car manufacturers would be required to make their cars odourless and noiseless. Only then could I enjoy fully the sensation of driving at its purest level.

But all this was turned upside down towards the end of 1973.

The Encounter

ON that extraordinary day – 13 December 1973 – I found myself in a crater of an Auvergne volcano, the Puy-de-Lassolas. There, as I have already described, I met for the first time an extra-terrestrial man or, more precisely, the Eloha – singular of Elohim – whom I would meet at the same place for six consecutive days and who, for about one hour each time, would dictate to me the fantastic revelations of the first part of this 'message'.

For the first few days following this experience I must confess I wondered if I would dare tell anyone at all about it. The first thing I did was to make a neat copy of the notes that I had taken as best I could, although far too quickly, as my interlocutor spoke to me. When this was finished, I sent the original manuscript to a serious publisher who to my knowledge did not publish esoteric works or science fiction. Obviously I did not want this message of such importance to humanity to be lost among collections of mysterious adventure stories or occult books that cater for people interested in alternative sciences.

Marcel Jullian, who ran the publishing house, invited me to Paris and told me that the manuscript was sensational. But he said that I must tell my life story before talking about the message, and that there might be 'a few little changes to be made.'

All that was absolutely out of the question. I did not want to take up a hundred pages telling my life story and then present the message that I had received, as if my personality were as important as those things which I had been asked to reveal. I wanted the message published, but only the message, even if it was not a thick book and thereby lacked interest for a publisher. So I asked Monsieur Jullian to return my manuscript. He replied that he did not have it, because a reader had borrowed it, but that as soon as it was returned he would mail it to me.

I had just returned to Clermont-Ferrand when I received a telegram inviting me to return to Paris to appear in a television show presented by the great chess master, Jacques Chancel. He was the director of a series in the publishing house to which I had sent my manuscript. He had read it and understood that it was absolutely fantastic, whether anyone believed it or not. So I took part in the show, and the thousands of letters that I received afterwards showed that, while some laughed, many had taken what I said very seriously and wanted to help.

But days went by and my manuscript was not returned. I sent a registered letter to the publisher, who replied that the manuscript would be sent to me, but that they had not yet found it. After ten days I went back to Paris to see if I could do something personally because nobody wanted to answer my questions any more when I telephoned to ask about the matter.

The famous designer, Courréges, who had contacted me after the television show because he was interested, agreed to come with me to see the publisher in order to find out what exactly had become of the manuscript. Marcel Jullian told us that the reader who had the manuscript had taken it with him on holiday but they did not know where he was or how to reach him. The situation was becoming stranger and stranger.

In the end the manuscript was retrieved by Monsieur Courréges and he returned it to me personally. I still wonder if it had really been lost, or just put away to prevent it from being published. If that publishing house really mislaid the manuscript so easily, then I would discourage other authors from sending their originals to them.

Alarmed by the mishap, and by the growing pile of letters from people interested in buying the book containing the message as soon as it was published, Marie-Paul offered to leave her nursing job to help me with the publishing and the distribution of this exceptional document.

I accepted, because I was sure that only in this way would I be able permanently to control the use to which these writings were put. Since it was incompatible with the seriousness of the mission that I had been given, I immediately stopped working for the sports magazine and in the autumn of 1974 the book finally rolled off the printing press.

The shock to my nervous system caused by this unforeseen upset in my life had given me stomach pains and almost brought on an ulcer. All winter I suffered from a serious case of gastritis. No medication was effective, and it was only after I decided to take it easy by doing some meditation and breathing exercises that the pains vanished as if by magic.

In June I had been on a television show hosted by Philippe Bouvard. It was called *Saturday Evening* and, sarcastic as always, Monsieur Bouvard disguised his co-host as a Martian, with pink antennae and a green suit, and asked me if he looked like the person I had met.

But many people, interested by the little I had been able to say, wrote to Philippe Bouvard, reproaching him for his lack of seriousness. Confronted by the thousands of letters he received, he decided to invite me back to do another show where I would be able to say a little more.

Convinced that I would not be allowed to say enough, I decided to hire the Pleyel Hall for a date just after the television show, and to announce to interested viewers that I would give a talk there in a few days' time. I hired a hall to seat 150 with an option on another to seat 500 as I did not know how many people would want to bother to come and listen to me.

In the end more than 3,000 people came. Quite obviously we could only accommodate 500 in the hall I had booked and when these seats were filled we advised the others that I would give another talk in a few days in the great hall with 2,000 seats. Obviously, many people were not happy to leave, some of them having travelled several hundred kilometres.

It all went well and I found that a great number of people were ready to help and support me, apart, of course, from those cynics whose questions, by virtue of their superficiality, I was able to show up as ridiculous.

Even though I had dreadful stage fright, much more than I had ever had when singing, everything went without a hitch, and the answers to the most difficult questions seemed to come to my lips by themselves. I really felt help coming from above, just as the Elohim had promised me. I had the impression of listening to myself give answers that I could not possibly have come up with alone.

The second talk took place a few days later. I was afraid that those who had not been able to get into the hall the first time would not come back and that I would therefore find myself stuck with a very expensive hall nearly three quarters empty. There had not been any publicity about it since the television programme, except for a short, three line paragraph in *France Soir*, the only newspaper that would agree to publicise this second talk.

In the event well over two thousand people came and the hall was full. It was a triumph. From this time onward, I did not have any further doubts about the success of my mission.

The Public Talks

FROM the month of September 1974 onwards, over the course of some forty lectures, I was able to see which questions came up most frequently. I also saw the membership of MADECH rising constantly as regional offices formed in all the big towns of France around the most dynamic and active members.

I also saw some reporters pursuing their craft honestly and well, their job being to inform the public by writing or saying exactly what they had seen or read about. However some, like those from the newspaper *Le*

Point, wrote lies. Even after registered letters were sent to remind them that they had to rectify an inaccurate article in conformity with the right to respond, they did not do so properly.

Others, like those at the newspaper *La Montagne,* simply refused to inform their readers that I was giving a talk in Clermont-Ferrand, and exploited the fact that they were the only daily newspaper in that region. Their news director had in fact met me and said that never would I or my activities be mentioned in his newspaper. All this was because they did not like the fact that when I appeared initially on television I had not first informed them before talking to a major French broadcasting organisation. A sad story and a fine example of freedom of speech. They even refused to run a paid advertisement announcing that talk, although in the same newspaper there were full-page advertisements for pornographic movies.

As for the newspaper *Le Point,* it simply transformed an excursion of MADECH members to the place where the encounter had occurred, into a broken appointment with the Elohim.

These tricks were played in an attempt to ridicule an organisation trying to get off the ground. It is evidently easier and less dangerous for a newspaper with an extensive readership to do this to a new organisation like MADECH than to the Church, with its 2,000 year history.

But the day will come when those who have tried to hide or twist the truth will regret their mistakes.

2

THE SECOND ENCOUNTER

The Sighting of 31 July 1975

IT was during June 1975 that I decided to resign as president of MADECH, first of all because it seemed that the movement could now manage very well without me, and secondly because I thought I had made a mistake in structuring the organisation in accordance with a 1901 law that likened the movement, which is of such importance to humanity, to a petanque club or a war veterans' association.

I thought it was necessary to create a movement more in harmony with the fantastic message the Elohim had transmitted to me. This required a movement that respected to the letter what our creators had advised – namely geniocracy, humanitarianism, the renunciation of all deistic religious practices, and so on.

Any association based on that 1901 law ran contrary to the meaning of the Elohim's message by definition, at least in the way we had structured it. Since all members of such an association could vote, we were not respecting the principles of geniocracy according to which only the most intelligent people may take part in making decisions. So I had to correct this fundamental mistake, not by going so far as to abolish MADECH, but rather to transform it, pending more effective modification of its structure. This would not run contrary to the regulations of the 1901 law.

In this way, MADECH would become an organisation that would support the real movement that I was going to create with its most open-minded members – in effect, a congregation of MADECH guides.

This new association would bring together those people who wished to open others' minds to infinity and eternity, and become guides for humanity by scrupulously applying what was required in the Elohim's message. So, in a society seeking to close people's minds in every way with deistic religions, soporific education, unthinking television programmes and petty political battles, I was going to try to initiate people who would go out into the world and attempt to open the minds of others. Thus MADECH would retain its importance by becoming a support organisation that would be the first point of contact for those discovering the Elohim's message. It would be made up of practising members, and the congregation of guides was going to be a movement made up of 'monks' guiding those practising members.

I knew that there were people among the MADECH members who were quite capable of managing the organisation, and I received confirmation of this during the elections to the administrative council. My replacement as president, Christian, was a physicist with a promising future, and the rest of the council was made up of people who were all equally representative and competent.

It was also in the month of June that François, one of the most devoted MADECH members and one of the most open-minded, came to see me in Clermont-Ferrand. I told him about my desire to find a country house in as secluded a place as possible, in order to rest a little and calmly write a book in which I would relate all that had happened to me prior to 13 December 1973 before anyone could invent a lot of nonsense about my past. He told me that he had a farm in an out of the way place in Périgord, and that if I liked the area I could spend a month or two there, and even stay as long as I wished, since nobody lived there.

We immediately drove off to visit the place and, inspired by the peace and quiet that I found there, I decided to stay for two months. After two weeks I was enjoying it so much that I seriously considered settling there more permanently.

François came back to join us at the end of July, and we started planning the move for the day after a celebration meeting at Clermont-Ferrand on 6 August. I still had not decided for sure, because I was afraid I might fail in my mission somehow if I moved away from the place of my marvellous encounter. However, on 31 July, while my wife Marie-Paul and François and I were out getting some fresh air, we saw what must have been an enormous craft passing silently and with jerky movements almost over the house.

At times it moved with unimaginable speed, but it also stopped suddenly several times, proceeding in a zigzag pattern like this about 500 metres from where we stood. I was delighted that other people were with me to witness the event, and an indescribable feeling of happiness came over me. François told me that the hairs on his head stood on end from emotion. To me, it was an obvious sign of the Elohim's consent to my moving to that area.

The next morning I noticed that I had a strange mark on the biceps of one arm, close to the fold of my elbow. I did not immediately make the connection to the sighting of the day before, but later many people told me that it could only have been a mark made by the Elohim. It was a red circle about three centimetres in diameter, its circumference was five millimetres thick and inside it were three smaller circles.

This mark stayed the same for the next two weeks, then the three circles in the middle merged into one, making two concentric circles. Then, after another two weeks, the two circles disappeared, leaving a white spot on my arm, which I still have. I wish to emphasise the fact that I never suffered from that mark, and that I did not feel the least itching during the entire time I had it. Some open-minded scientists to whom I showed the mark speculated that it could have been made while a sample was being taken with the help of a perfected laser.

The reunion of 6 August finally took place as planned in the crater of Puy-de-Lassolas, near Clermont-Ferrand and at that the meeting a splendid feeling of fraternity and harmony prevailed.

I had decided to hold this gathering of MADECH members on this date without really knowing why, but in fact the Elohim had guided me, because on the day of the meeting some members informed me that it was the thirtieth anniversary to the day of the atomic bomb explosion at Hiroshima, and that it was also a Christian holiday, the Transfiguration. Fools will say that it was a coincidence.

After that meeting, some MADECH members helped me to move, and I settled down to live in Périgord.

The Message: Part Two

ON 7 October, at around eleven o'clock at night, I felt a sudden urge to go out and look at the sky. I dressed warmly because it was rather cool, and set out walking in the dark. I was going in a certain direction without being conscious of it, and suddenly felt the need to go to a spot that François had shown me during the summer – a deserted place between two brooks and surrounded by forest. It was called the Roc Plat. I reached it around midnight half wondering what I was doing there, but following my intuition since I had been told that I could be guided telepathically.

The sky was magnificent and stars were shining everywhere for there was not a single cloud to be seen. As I stood watching the shooting stars, the whole countryside suddenly lit up, and I saw a huge ball of fire appear behind some bushes. I moved toward the place where the ball of fire had appeared, filled with a tremendous joy, as I was almost certain of what I was going to find.

The same craft that I had seen on six occasions in the month of December 1973 was there in front of me, and the same person I had met two years earlier came towards me with a smile full of kindness. I noticed one difference right away. He no longer had on the spacesuit that had seemed to make a halo around his face the first time. After all the time I had spent trying to make the world understand that I was indeed telling the truth, I was wonderfully happy to see once more the person who had been responsible for turning my life upside down. I bowed before him, and he spoke.

'Stand up, and follow me,' he said. 'We are very satisfied with you and with everything you have done for the past two years. It is now time to pass on to the next stage, since you have proven to us that we can trust you. These two years were in fact just a trial. You can see that today I have no protection around my face, and that my craft appeared to you all at once and was not equipped with flashing lights. All of that was only intended to reassure you, so that I would appear in a way that corresponds to the image that you generally have of space travellers. But now that you are sufficiently evolved not to take fright, we won't use such approach techniques any more.'

Following him inside the craft, I noticed that its interior looked very

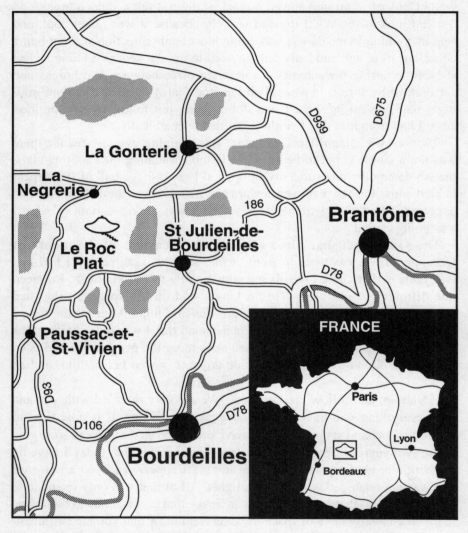

Site of Raël's second encounter – Le Roc Plat, near Brantôme, Périgord region, 7 October 1975.

similar to what I had found at our first meeting – walls with the same metallic appearance as the outside, no control board or instruments, no portholes, and a floor made of a translucent blue substance on which stood two armchairs. These were made of a transparent material that reminded me a little of inflatable plastic chairs, but without feeling unpleasant.

He invited me to sit down in one of the two chairs, settled into the other, and asked me not to move. He then pronounced a few words in an incomprehensible language, and I seemed to feel the machine rock slightly. Then all of a sudden, I felt a sensation of severe cold, as if my whole body were turning into a block of ice, or rather as if thousands of ice crystals were penetrating all the pores of my skin, right down to the marrow of my bones. It lasted a very short time, a few seconds perhaps, and I felt nothing after that.

Then my companion rose and said: 'You may come, we have arrived.'

I followed him down the small stairway. The craft stood motionless in a metallic-looking circular room about fifteen metres in diameter and ten metres high. A door opened, and my guide told me to go in and undress completely. After that I would receive further instructions. I went into a new circular room that did not have the slightest angle, and must have been about four metres in diameter. I undressed, and a voice told me to go into the room that was in front of me.

At that moment a door opened, and I went into a room similar to the one where I had left my clothes, but it was long and a little like a corridor. Along the length of that corridor I passed under lights of different colours in turn. The voice then told me that by following the arrows painted on the floor, I would arrive in yet another room where a bath awaited me.

In this next room I did indeed find a sunken bathtub. The water was lukewarm, just right, and discreetly perfumed. The voice advised me to satisfy my personal needs, which I did, and then it asked me to drink the contents of a glass located on a small shelf by the metallic wall. It was a white liquid deliciously flavoured with almonds, and very cold. Then some soft, pyjama-like clothes that felt like silk were offered to me. They were white, very close fitting, and had been laid out ready for me on another shelf. At last a final door opened and I found my guide again. He was escorted by two people who were of similar appearance to him but with different features, and they were every bit as welcoming.

I rejoined them in a huge hall where I found wonder after wonder. It was arranged on several levels and must have measured 100 metres in diameter. It was covered by an absolutely transparent dome, so transparent that at first sight it was not clear even that it was a dome. Thousands of stars studded the dark sky, and yet the entire hall was brightly lit with a soft, natural-looking light, as if it were midday. The floor was covered with furs and shaggy carpets of astounding, enchanting colours. The most admirable works of art were everywhere, each one more beautiful than the last, and some had animated and changing colours. Elsewhere there were plants – some bright red and others blue, as beautiful as exotic fish but several metres tall. Background music was playing that sounded like an organ and a musical saw, with occasional choirs and bass voices producing extraordinary vibrations.

This music made the flowers bend and sway in rhythm and they changed colours with each change of musical style.

Every time someone spoke, the music grew softer so that we could hear each other without difficulty and without having to raise our voices. The air was perfumed with a thousand scents that also changed with the music and our positions in the room. The whole area had been designed with about ten angled corners, which were separated at different levels and each corner had a particular character. A small stream meandered through all this.

My guide's two companions were showing him great respect and the next thing he said to me was: 'Follow me. We shall make ourselves comfortable, since I have many things to tell you.'

I followed him to a group of armchairs and sofas made of a very soft black fur, where all four of us sat down. There my guide spoke again:

'TODAY I am going to give you a second message that will complete the one that I dictated to you in December 1973. You don't have anything to take notes with, but don't worry, everything that I say to you will remain engraved in your mind, because here we have a technique that allows you to remember everything you hear.

First of all, we wish to congratulate you for all that you have done over the past two years, but we also wish to warn you that the rest of your mission may be more difficult. But never be discouraged in any case, because you will be rewarded for your efforts, whatever happens now.

To begin with, we must correct a passage in the first message we gave you that you wrongly transcribed concerning an eventual intervention on our part to destroy humanity. It must be made clear that we will not intervene. Humanity is now arriving at a turning point in its history, and its future depends only on itself. If you can control your aggressiveness towards each other and your environment, then you will reach a golden age of interplanetary civilisation, in which universal happiness and fulfilment will be realised. If, on the other hand, your civilisation gives way to violence, then it will destroy itself, either directly or indirectly through all this.

No scientific or technical problem is insurmountable for human genius, as long as human genius is in control. But someone with a deficient brain can threaten worldwide peace, just as a person of genius can bring the world happiness.

The sooner you set up geniocracy, the sooner you will remove the possibility of a cataclysm caused by people with minds that are not very evolved. In the event of a cataclysm destroying humanity, only the people who follow you will be saved, and they will have to repopulate the devastated Earth when all the danger has been dispersed, as happened in Noah's time.'

Buddhism

MY guide paused briefly, then he continued:

'Buddhism explains that at the time of death, the soul of the dead person must be vigilant enough to escape numerous devils, otherwise it will be reincarnated and fall back into the cycle. On the other hand, if it manages to escape those infamous devils, it will be liberated from the cycle and attain a state of bliss through awakening.

In fact, this is a very good description which applies not to the individual but to humanity as a whole. It must resist those devils, which can make it fall back into the cycle each time it is in a position to choose. Those 'devils' are aggressiveness directed against our fellow human beings or against nature and the 'state of bliss through awakening' is a golden age of civilisation in which science serves the people, thus producing an earthly paradise, where the blind can see and the deaf can hear by scientific means.

If humanity is not sufficiently wary of these devils, it will fall back into the cycle of reincarnation, where it must start all over again from a primitive state and advance progressively towards a more evolved society in a hostile world, with all the suffering which that entails.

That is why the swastika figures in our symbol, as in numerous ancient writings, symbolising this cycle. It is the choice between paradise, which the peaceful use of science makes possible, and the hell of returning to the primitive stage where humanity submits to nature instead of dominating and benefiting from it.

In a way, this is natural selection at the cosmic level for species that are capable of leaving their planet. Only those who perfectly control their aggressiveness can reach this stage. The others self destruct as soon as their scientific and technological levels permit them to invent weapons powerful enough to do so. That is why we never fear those who come from elsewhere to contact us. Thousands of contacts have confirmed this absolute rule in the universe – people capable of escaping their planetary system are always peaceful.

When a species is capable of leaving its own solar system it means that it has overcome the 'progress-destruction cycle' that can occur when mastery of its own aggressive tendencies is lacking. At the same time that you discover powerful energy sources allowing you to travel beyond your own solar system, you also become capable of creating offensive weapons of irreversible destructive power.

Your region of the terrestrial globe, France, is already on the right track in its attempt to unite Europe, and it should be the first country without an army. France would thus set an example for the entire world. Its military professionals would then lay the foundation for a peace-keeping European army, eventually transforming it into a world peace corps. Instead of being the guardians of war, the military would then be the guardians of peace, a title deserving infinitely more respect.

It is necessary for an important country to show the way for others to follow, and France's neighbouring countries will not invade her just because she has abolished compulsory military service and is using her professional army in the service of the Europe that she is trying to construct.

On the contrary, this would very quickly cause other countries to follow suit and pursue the same path taken by your country. Once Europe is united militarily, its economy can be united by creating a single European currency. Then the same process could be applied throughout the world, adding as we have already told you in the first message, a single world language that would become compulsory in every school on Earth. If one country must show the way, then France is that country. It is by advocating 'a deterrent force' that we accumulate the arms of our own destruction.

With each country wishing to deter some other country, and in practice never quite knowing which one, an unfortunate action could then threaten to transform that 'deterrent force' into a force of intervention, which could be fatal to the whole world.

It is through the past that humanity views the future. This is a mistake. We should instead be critical of the past and build the present for the future rather than build the present on the basis of the past. You must understand that barely thirty years ago, people of countries that are now advanced were still primitive. You are only just emerging. There are millions of people on Earth who are still primitive and incapable of seeing something in the sky as anything other than a 'divine' manifestation. Moreover, you know that deistic religions are still very strong in all the economically less-developed countries.

You must not revere people for their age, but for their intelligence, while seeing to it that old people have a pleasant life. Our distant ancestors should not be respected and furthermore they should be seen as an example of poor, limited, primitive people who were unable to open themselves to the universe and who were incapable of handing down very much of value from one generation to the next.'

Neither God nor Soul

MY guide went on to say:

'The more primitive a society is, the more deistic religions will flourish within it. These religions are actually cultivated by visitors from other planets, who have no other way of peacefully visiting worlds that have not yet overcome their aggressiveness.

If you reach the stage where you become evolved visitors on primitive worlds, you will be forced to use such a system, which is in fact very amusing and involves passing yourselves off as gods in their eyes. In fact, this is extremely easy since, for primitive people, if you come from the sky you can only be divine. Of course, you must lay it on a bit thick to be respected and pleasantly received, which does no harm. We continue to make appearances on Earth to see if this still works and to see the reactions of public authorities, governments, and the press. We often amuse ourselves quite a lot . . .

As we have already explained to you in the first part of this message, there is no God, and obviously, no soul. After death there is nothing, unless science is used to create something. As you know, it is possible to recreate a dead organism from one of the organism's cells, which contains its physical and intellectual blueprint. We have noted that an organism loses a few grams at the moment of its death – in fact this is merely the energy that all living things have available to them, which is eliminated at that moment. As you know, energy, like matter, has weight.

You also know that we have discovered that there is organised, intelligent life on the level of the infinitely small, quite certainly as evolved as we are and comparable to what we are ourselves.

We have been able to prove this.

From there, we have discovered that the stars and planets are the atoms of a gigantic being, which itself certainly contemplates other stars with curiosity. It is also highly likely that the people living on the infinitely small levels of the infinitely large person and its fellow creatures have known periods when they believed in an immaterial "God".

You must fully understand that everything is in everything. At this moment in an atom of your arm, millions of worlds are being born and others are dying, believing or not believing in a "God" and a soul, and when a millennium has gone by for you, the gigantic being of whom the sun is an atom has only had the time to take one step.

Time is, in fact, inversely proportional to the mass or, rather to the level of the form of life. But everything in the universe is alive and in harmony with the infinitely large and the infinitely small.

The Earth is alive like all the planets, and for the small growth that is humanity it is difficult to notice this, because of the time lag due to the enormous difference in mass, which prevents you from perceiving its palpitations. Nor could one of our red blood cells or, better still, one of the atoms that make up our body imagine that it forms, with its peers, a living being.

Finally, whatever happens to each individual, the universal balance remains constant. But if we want to be happy at our level, we must live in harmony with the infinitely large, the infinitely small, and with our fellow human beings.

No argument aiming to support the existence of any type of god or soul can be sustained when we glimpse, however briefly, the infinite nature of the universe. No heaven could exist in any particular place because, since the universe is infinite, it cannot have a centre. Besides, as I have already explained, there cannot be any communication between an infinitely large entity and a universe of infinitely small entities, because the difference in mass is too great, thus creating a difference in the flow of equivalent time.

Finally, if one can imagine an immortal soul escaping from the body after death – an image that is very poetic but rather naive since it comes from the minds of primitives – one cannot imagine where it would go, given that the universe is infinite.

The quantity of energy that flies off at the time of death disperses in a random way, losing all identity as it blends with all the energies suspended in the surrounding air. That identity is obviously engraved only in organised matter, such as the cells of a living being that has just died. This matter is organised according to the blueprint which the genes of the male and the female determined at conception while creating the first cell.

With regard to the origin of life on Earth, some people might say: "Your explanation doesn't change a thing, since you cannot say what there was at the very beginning."

This is a foolish comment which proves that the person who makes it has no awareness of infinity that exists in time as well as in space. There is neither a beginning nor an end to matter since "nothing is lost, nothing is created, everything is transformed," as you have already heard it said. Only the form of matter can change according to the wishes of those who have reached a scientific level which allows them to accomplish this.

It is the same for the infinite levels of life. That is what the second part of our emblem represents. The Star of David, which is composed of two intertwined triangles, means "as above, so below." With the swastika, which signifies that everything is cyclic, in the middle of a six pointed star, you have our emblem, which contains all the wisdom in the world. You can also find the two symbols together in ancient writings like the *Bardo Thodol* or Tibetan *Book of the Dead,* and in many other writings as well.

It is evidently very difficult for a finite human brain to be conscious of infinity, which explains the need to limit the universe in time and space by belief in one or several gods that are made responsible for everything.

Indeed, those who cannot reach a sufficient level of human understanding towards the universe have trouble accepting the notion of infinity, which makes humanity nothing exceptional, but merely people situated at a particular time and place in the infinite universe.

People obviously prefer things to be well defined, well framed, limited in a way, in the image of their own minds. Those who ask themselves if it is possible that there is life on other planets are the best example of those limited minds, and we liked very much the comparison you made during one of your lectures, likening such people to frogs at the bottom of their own pond wondering whether there was life in other ponds.'

Paradise on Earth

'YOU could very soon live in a genuine terrestrial paradise if only the technology that you have at your disposal today were made to serve human well-being, instead of serving violence, armies, or the personal profit of a few.

Science and technology can totally liberate humanity not only from the problem of hunger in the world, but also from the obligation to work to live, since machines can quite easily look after the daily chores by themselves thanks to automation.

Already, in some of your most modern factories where it used to take several hundred people to build one car, now only a single individual is needed to oversee a computer that commands and carries out all the car-building operations. In the future, even that one person will be unnecessary. Workers' unions are not happy about this, because factories are in less and less need of personnel and are letting more and more workers go. Still, the unions are wrong – these fantastic machines which do the work of 500 people should enable those 500 to really live, rather than enrich only one person, their boss.

No individual should be in the service of another, nor work for anyone for a salary. Machines can easily do all the chores and take care of all the work, enabling people to dedicate themselves to the one thing for which they were created – to think, create and blossom. That is what happens on our planet. Your children must no longer be raised according to the three primitive precepts of work, family, country. On the contrary, they should be brought up following the principles of development, freedom, universal fraternity.

"Work" is not sacred when it is motivated only by the need to earn just enough to live a laborious life of hardship. It is even terribly degrading to sell oneself, and one's life, in order to eat, by doing jobs which simple machines could do.

The "family" has never been anything but a way for ancient as well as modern supporters of slavery to force people to work harder for an illusory ideal.

Finally, "patriotism" is still only a supplementary means of creating competition between people and urging them to perform their sacrosanct work with greater ardour each day.

What is more, those three concepts – work, family, country – have always been supported by primitive religions. But now you are no longer primitive people. Shake off all those dusty old principles and make the most of your life on Earth, which science can transform into paradise

Do not be taken in by those who speak to you of potential enemies and allow armament factories to compel underpaid workers to produce destructive weapons that bring profits to big industrialists. Do not be taken in by those who speak to you in horror of the falling birthrate, because young people understand that they need not have so many children, and that it is better to have fewer so they can be happier.

Do not be taken in by those who constantly brandish remarks under your nose, saying things like "neighbouring peoples are multiplying and could become a threat." They are the same people who support the stockpiling of nuclear weapons under the pretext of "deterrence".

Finally, do not let yourself be taken in by those who tell you that military service enables you to learn how to use a gun and that "it can always be useful", while they continue to pile up nuclear missiles.

They want to teach you violence, to teach you not to be afraid of killing a person like yourself, using the excuse that he is wearing a different uniform, and training you until it becomes a mechanical reflex after repeated practice against training targets.

Do not be taken in by those who tell you that you must fight for your country. No country deserves it. Do not be influenced by those who say to you: "What if enemies invade our country, shouldn't we defend ourselves?" Answer that non-violence is always more efficient than violence. It is not proven that those who died for France were right, no matter how hostile their aggressors were. Look at the triumph of Gandhi in India.

Such people will tell you that you must fight for your liberty, but they forget that the Gauls lost their war against the Romans and that the French are no worse off for being descendants of the conquered, having benefited from the civilisation of the conquerors. Live rather in fulfilment, freedom and love, instead of listening to all those narrow-minded, aggressive people.

The most important aid you have to help you reach a long and lasting universal peace is television, the source of a genuine planetary awareness that makes it possible to see what goes on every day all over the globe, and realise that the "barbarians" who live on the other side of the border have all the same joys, the same sorrows and the same problems as yourselves. It also records the progress of science, the latest artistic creations, and so on.

Of course, it is important to ensure that this wonderful tool of diffusion and communication does not fall into the hands of people who would use it to condition the mass of the people by providing biased information.

You really can consider television to be the nervous system of humanity, which enables each individual to be aware of the existence of others and to see how they live. It also prevents the spread of distorted ideas about others that create a fear of strangers. Long ago there was fear of the neighbouring tribe, then fear of the neighbouring village, of the neighbouring province, and of the neighbouring state.

There is currently a fear of the neighbouring race, and if this no longer existed, there would be fear of potential aggressors coming from another planet.

It is necessary to reverse this attitude and be open to everything that comes from the outside, because all fear of strangers is proof of a primitive level of civilisation. In this sense television is irreplaceable, and is possibly the most important development of any civilisation because, in the same way as radio, it enables all those isolated cells of humanity, which people are, to be informed at all times of what the others are doing. As already indicated it works exactly as the nervous system does in the body of a living being.'

The Other World

'YOU are probably wondering where you are,' my guide said. 'In fact you are now on a base located relatively close to the Earth. In the first message you noted that we travelled seven times faster than the speed of light. That was true 25,000 years ago when we landed on Earth. Since then, we have made much progress and we now travel through space much faster. It only takes us a few moments to make the journey that used to take us almost two months in those times, and we continue to progress. If you will now follow me, we will take a little trip together.'

I rose and followed my three guides. We went through an airlock, and in a vast room I noticed a craft similar to the one that had brought me from Earth, but it was far larger. The exterior must have been about twelve metres in diameter, and inside it had four seats facing each other instead of just two. We sat down as before, and again I felt the same sensation of intense cold but it lasted much longer this time – about ten minutes. Then the craft rocked slightly, and we stepped out through the trap door exit.

Before me a paradisial landscape unfolded, and in fact I cannot find any words to describe my enchantment at seeing huge flowers, each more beautiful than the last, and animals of unimaginable appearance that were walking among them. There were birds with multicoloured plumage, and pink and blue squirrels with the heads of bear cubs climbing in the branches of trees that bore both enormous fruits and gigantic flowers.

About thirty metres from the spacecraft, a small group of Elohim was waiting for us, and behind the trees I was able to make out a group of buildings that resembled brightly coloured shells harmonising perfectly with the vegetation. The temperature was very mild, and the air was perfumed with countless scents of exotic flowers. We walked towards the top of a hill, and a marvellous panorama began to appear. Innumerable small streams wound through the lush vegetation, and far off an azure sea sparkled in the sun.

Reaching a clearing, I discovered with great astonishment a group of people similar to me, by which I mean people resembling those who live on Earth, not Elohim. Most of them were naked or wore robes made of multicoloured silks. They bowed respectfully before my three guides, and then we all sat down.

Our armchairs seemed to have been carved in the rock and were covered with thick furs that always remained fresh and comfortable despite the warmth. Some people came out of a small cave located right next to us and approached, carrying trays piled high with fruits, grilled meats accompanied by the most incredible sauces, and drinks of unforgettable flavours.

Behind each guest two of the men who carried the trays were kneeling ready to satisfy the slightest wish of those who were eating. The latter would ask them for whatever they desired without even looking at them. During the meal some marvellous music had started up, from where I could not tell, and young naked women with figures as sculptural as those of the waiters started to dance with incomparable grace on the surrounding lawn.

There must have been some forty guests who were similar to people from Earth in addition to my three guides. There were white, yellow and black men and women who all spoke a language I could not understand that resembled Hebrew.

I was sitting to the right of the Eloha whom I had met two years earlier, and to the left of the two other Elohim. Facing me sat a young bearded man, very handsome and very slim. He wore a mysterious smile and an expression filled with fraternal feeling. To his right was a man with a noble face sporting a black beard that was very thick and very long. To his left was a more corpulent man with an Asian face. He had a shaven head.

Meeting the Ancient Prophets

TOWARDS the end of the meal my guide again spoke to me.

'In my first message I told you of a residence located on our planet where people from Earth can continue to live thanks to the scientific secret of eternity that is based on a single cell.

Among those people are Jesus, Moses, Elijah and so on. This residence is, in fact, very large, since it is an entire planet where the members of the Council of the Eternals live as well. My name is Yahweh, and I am the president of that Council of the Eternals.

There are currently 8,400 people from Earth living on the planet where we are at this moment. They are people who during their lives reached a sufficient level of open-mindedness toward the infinite, or who enabled humanity on Earth to progress from its primitive level through their discoveries, their writings, their ways of organising society and their exemplary acts of fraternity, love or selflessness. Alongside them live the 700 Elohim members of the Council of the Eternals.

Whatever the outcome of your mission may be, you have your place reserved here among us in this veritable little paradise where everything is easy, thanks to science, and where we live happily and eternally. I can truly say eternally, for, as on Earth, we created all life here, and we are starting to understand perfectly the life of the infinitely large, that is to say, of the planets, and we can detect signs of old age in solar systems, which will enable us to leave this planet in time to create another paradise elsewhere, as soon as we grow anxious about its survival.

The eternals who live here, both people from Earth and Elohim, can fulfil themselves as they wish, without having to do anything but that which pleases them – scientific research, meditation, music, painting, and so on. Or they can do nothing at all if they feel like it.

The servants you saw carrying the dishes a little while ago, as well as the dancers, are just biological robots. They are created according to the same principle we used to create the people of Earth in a totally scientific way. They are limited by their own choice and absolutely submissive to us.

They are also incapable of acting without orders from us, and they are very specialised. They have no aspirations of their own, and no desires for pleasure, except certain ones that their specialisations require. They grow old and die like us, but the machine that makes them can make far more than we need. They are incapable of feelings or suffering, and cannot reproduce themselves.

Their life span is similar to ours – that is to say about 700 years with the help of a small surgical intervention. When one of them must be destroyed due to old age, the machine that created them produces one or several others, depending on our needs. They come out of the machine ready to function and with their normal height, for they have neither growth nor childhood. They only know how to do one thing: obey people from Earth and Elohim, and they are incapable of the slightest violence.

They can all be recognised by the small blue stone that both males and females wear between their eyes. They take care of the dirty jobs and do all the work that is uninteresting. They are produced, taken care of and destroyed underground, where, in fact, all the maintenance work is done by such robots and by enormous computers that regulate all the problems of nourishment, supply of raw materials, energy and other things. We each have on average ten robots at our service, and as there are slightly more than 9,000 of us – Earth people and Elohim – there is a permanent total of 90,000 male and female robots.

Like the Elohim members of the Council of the Eternals, the eternals from Earth are not allowed to have children. They agree to have a small operation which makes them sterile, but that sterility can easily be reversed. The purpose of this measure is to prevent undeserving beings from joining us in this marvellous world. However, male and female eternals can unite freely just as they wish, and all jealousy is eliminated.

In addition, men who wish to have one or more companions outside the relationships of equality that exist between eternal men and women, or who do not want to live with a woman on an equal basis, may have one or more totally submissive biological robot women with the exact appearance that is desired. The same goes for women, who can have one or several totally submissive biological robot men.

The machine that generates the robots gives the entity that it creates the exact physical appearance and specialisation desired. There are several types of ideal women and men in terms of shape and physiognomy, but the height, measurements, shape of the face, and so on, can be modified as one wishes. One can even submit the picture of someone particularly admired or loved on Earth, for example, and the machine will produce an exact replica. Thus the relationships between eternals of both sexes are much more fraternal and respectful, and the unions between them are marvellously pure and high.

Because of the extraordinary level of open-mindedness of those admitted here, there is never any problem between them. The majority spend almost all of their time meditating, doing scientific research, making inventions and artistic compositions, and creating all sorts of things. We can live in different cities with multiple architectural styles in greatly varied sites that we can modify at will. People fulfil themselves as they wish, only doing what they like to do.

Some find pleasure in doing scientific experiments, others in playing music, others in creating ever more amazing animals, and others in meditating or doing nothing other than making love while enjoying the numerous pleasures of this heavenly environment, drinking from the innumerable fountains and eating the juicy fruits that grow all over the place at all times. Here there is no winter; we all live in a region comparable to your equator, but as we can scientifically control the climate, it is always fine weather and not too hot. We make the rain fall during the night when and where we wish. All this, and many other things which you could not understand all at once, make this world a true paradise. Here, everyone is free and totally safe, for all deserve that liberty.

All things that bring pleasure are positive, as long as that pleasure is not harmful to anyone in any way. This is why all sensual pleasure is positive, for sensuality is always an opening up to the outside world, and all such opening is good. On Earth you are only just emerging from all those primitive taboos that tried to make anything to do with sex or nudity appear evil, whereas nothing could possibly be purer.

Nothing is more disappointing for your creators than to hear people say that nudity is something bad: nudity, the image of what we have made. As you can see, almost everyone is naked here; and those dressed in clothes wear them either because they are works of art given to them by other eternals who made them with their own hands, or for elegance and decoration.

When people from Earth are admitted to this world of the eternals, they start out by receiving some chemical education so that nothing surprises them, and they have a good understanding of where they are and why.'

My guide, Yahweh, paused for a moment, and then said:'You are now sitting directly opposite the man who, 2,000 years ago, was given the responsibility of creating a movement to spread more widely the message

147

we had left originally to the people of Israel – a message which would enable you to be understood now. I am referring to Jesus, whom we were able to recreate from a cell that we had preserved before his crucifixion.'

The handsome, bearded, young man seated opposite offered me a smile full of fraternity.

'To his right is Moses, to his left Elijah, and to the left of Elijah sits the one remembered on Earth by the name of Buddha. A little further on you can see Muhammed, in whose writings I am called Allah, because out of respect they did not dare call me by name. The forty men and women present at this meal are all representatives of the religions created after our contacts on Earth.'

All those present looked at me with expressions that were very friendly and amused, probably because they were remembering their own surprise upon arriving in this world.

My guide continued, 'Now I will show you some of our installations.'

He rose and I followed him. He invited me to put on a very wide belt bearing a huge buckle. He and his two friends had buckled on the same kind of adornment. Immediately I felt myself being lifted up from the ground and carried at about twenty metres above the grass, almost level with the tops of the trees, at a very great speed, probably over sixty miles per hour. My three companions were with me, Yahweh in front and his two friends behind. One curious thing, among others, was that I did not feel any wind at all whipping against my face.

We landed in a small clearing, quite close to the entrance of a small cave. We were in fact still being carried by our belts, but only at a height of one metre above the ground, and moving more slowly. We passed through galleries with metallic walls and arrived in a vast hall, in the centre of which was an enormous machine surrounded by about ten robots recognisable by the ornaments on their foreheads. There we landed on the ground again, and took off our belts.

Yahweh then spoke: 'Here is the machine that makes biological robots. We are going to create one of them for you.'

He made a sign to one of the robots located near the machine, and the robot touched certain parts of it. Then he made a sign for me to move close to a window measuring about two metres by one metre. In a bluish liquid I then saw the form of a human skeleton vaguely taking shape. Its form grew clearer and clearer, finally becoming a real skeleton. Then some nerves took shape and formed over the bones, then some muscles and finally some skin and hair. A splendid athlete was now lying there in a position where moments earlier there had been nothing.

Yahweh spoke again: 'Remember in the Old Testament this description in Ezekiel, Chapter 37: *"Son of man, can these bones live? . . . There was a noise, and behold a shaking, and the bones came together, bone to his bone. And when I beheld, lo, the sinews and the flesh came up upon them, and the skin covered them above...and the breath came into them, and they lived, and stood up upon their feet, an exceeding great army."* The description that you will give of this will certainly be similar to Ezekiel's – apart from the noise, which we have been able to eliminate.'

Indeed, what I had seen corresponded perfectly to Ezekiel's description. Following this, the prostrate figure had slid to the left and disappeared completely from my sight. Then a trap door opened, and I saw the creature whose rapid creation I had witnessed, lying on a very white fabric.

He was still immobile, but suddenly he opened his eyes, got up, came down the few steps that separated him from our level and, after exchanging a few words with another robot, came up to me. He gave me his hand, which I shook, and I felt his skin soft and warm.

'Do you have a picture of a loved one with you?' Yahweh asked.

'Yes,' I answered, 'I have a picture of my mother in my wallet, which I left in my clothes.'

He showed it to me, asking if it was the right one. When I agreed that it was, he gave it to one of the robots, who inserted it in the machine and touched parts of it. Through the window I witnessed yet another creation of a living being. Then, as the skin started to cover the flesh, I realised what was happening: they were making an exact replica of my mother from the picture I had provided . . .Indeed, a few moments later I was able to kiss my mother, or rather the image of my mother as she had been ten years before, for the picture I had provided had been taken about ten years previously.

Yahweh then said to me: 'Now allow us to make a very small puncture in your forehead.'

One of the robots came towards me, and with the help of a small device similar to a syringe, pricked my forehead so lightly that I hardly felt it. Then he inserted the syringe in the enormous machine and touched other parts of it. Again an entity was formed before my eyes. As the skin covered the flesh, I saw another 'me' take shape, little by little. Indeed, the being that emerged from the machine was an exact replica of myself.

'As you can see,' Yahweh told me, 'this other you is not wearing the small stone on his forehead that is characteristic of the robots and which the replica of your mother also had.

'From a photo we can only make a replica of the physical body, with no psychological personality or almost none, whereas from a sample cell like the one we took from between your eyes we can create a total replication of the individual whose cell we took, complete with the memory, personality and character. We could now send the other you back to Earth and people would not notice a thing. But we are going to destroy this replica immediately, for it is of no use to us.

'At this moment there are two of you who are listening to me, and the personalities of these two beings are beginning to be different, because you know that you are going to live and he knows that he is going to be destroyed. But that does not bother him, since he knows he is nothing but yourself. This is more proof, if proof is needed, of the non-existence of the soul – or a purely spiritual entity unique to each body – in which certain primitive people believe.'

After that we left the room that housed that enormous machine, and through a corridor we entered another room containing other equipment. We approached another machine.

'In this machine are kept the cells of malevolent people who will be recreated to be judged when the time comes. They are cells from those on Earth who preached violence, wickedness, aggressiveness and obscurantism. Despite having in their possession all the elements to understand where they came from, these people did not have the sense to recognise the truth. They will be recreated to undergo the punishment they deserve after being judged by those whom they made to suffer, or by their ancestors or descendants.

'You now fully deserve a rest. This robot will be your guide and will provide you with anything you desire until tomorrow morning. We will then have a few more words to say to you, and afterwards we will accompany you back to Earth. Between now and then you will have a foretaste of what awaits you when your mission is completed on your planet.'

The next moment a robot approached and saluted me re
was tall, athletic looking, dark, beardless and very handsome

A Foretaste of Paradise

THE robot asked me if I wanted to see my room, and after I agreed, he handed me one of the belts used for travelling. I found myself being transported above the ground again, and when I landed once more I found myself in front of a house that looked more like a scallop shell than a residence. The interior was entirely carpeted with shaggy furs, and there was a huge bed, at least as big as four Earth beds, looking as if it had been sunk into the ground. It was recognisable only by the different coloured furs covering it. In one corner of the huge room there was a massive sunken bathtub as big as a swimming pool surrounded by vegetation of marvellous shapes and colours.

'Would you like some female companions?' asked the robot. 'Come, you can make your own choice.'

I put my belt on again and found myself transported back in front of the machine used for making robots. A luminous cube appeared in front of me. I was shown to an armchair facing the cube and given a helmet.

When I had settled down, a magnificent young brunette with marvellously harmonious proportions appeared three-dimensionally within the luminous cube. She moved in such a way as to show herself off, and had she not been in a cube floating one metre above the ground, I would have thought she was real.

My robot asked me whether she pleased me and if I wished to have her shape altered or her face modified. I told him that I considered her perfect. He replied that aesthetically speaking she was the ideal woman, or rather one of the three types of ideal woman as defined by the computer according to the taste of the majority of residents on the planet. But I could ask for any modification that I desired.

At my refusal to change anything whatsoever about that magnificent creature, a second woman, this time blonde and alluring, appeared in the luminous cube. She was different but just as perfect as the first one. With her I could not find anything to alter, either. Finally, a third young female, _his one a red-head more sensual than the first two, appeared in the strange cube. The robot asked me if I cared to see other models, or if these three ideal types of my race would be enough for me. I answered quite naturally that I thought these three people were extraordinary.

At that moment, a magnificent black woman appeared in the cube, then a very fine slender Chinese female, and then finally another voluptuous young Asian woman.

The robot asked me which person I desired to have as a companion. Since I answered that they all pleased me, he went towards the robot making machine and spoke for a moment with one of his peers. Then the machine was set in motion, and I understood what was about to happen.

A few minutes later I was back at my residence with my six companions. There I had the most unforgettable bath that I have ever had, in the company of those charming robots, totally submissive to all my desires. Afterwards my robot guide asked if I wished to make some music. When I said 'yes', he took out a helmet similar to the one I had put on before the projection of the female robot models.

'Now,' he said, 'imagine some music that you would like to hear.'

Immediately a sound was heard, corresponding exactly to music that I had been thinking about, and as I constructed a melody in my head, that same melody became a reality with sounds of an amplitude and a sensitivity that were more extraordinary than any I had ever heard. The dream of every composer had become a reality – the ability to compose music directly without having to go through the laborious process of writing and orchestrating.

Then my six adorable companions began dancing to my music in a most voluptuous and bewitching way.

After a while, my robot asked me if I would also care to compose some images. Another helmet was given to me and I sat in front of a semi-circular screen. I set myself to imagining certain scenes and these scenes at once became visible on the screen. I was seeing, in fact, an immediate visualisation of all the thoughts that came to me. I started thinking about my grandmother, and she appeared on the screen. I thought of a bouquet of flowers and it appeared, and when I imagined a rose with green spots, it appeared as well. This machine actually made it possible to visualise one's thoughts instantaneously without having to explain them. What a marvel!

'With training one can create a story and have it played out,' my robot told me. 'Many performances of this kind, performances of direct creation, are held here.'

Finally, after a while, I went to bed and spent the most extravagant night of my life with my marvellous female companions.

The next day I got up, took another perfumed bath, and then a robot served us a delicious breakfast. Then he asked me to follow him, for Yahweh was expecting me. I put on the transportation belt again, and soon found myself in front of a strange machine, where the president of the Council of the Eternals was waiting for me.

It was not as large as the one which created robots, but was still very big. A sizable armchair was embedded in its centre.

Yahweh asked me if I had spent a pleasant night, and then explained to me: 'This machine will awaken certain faculties that lie dormant within you. Your brain will then be able to exploit its full potential. Sit down here.'

I sat down in the chair that he indicated and a sort of shell covered my skull. I thought I was losing consciousness for a moment, and then it felt as if my head were about to explode.

I saw multicoloured flashes pass before my eyes. Finally everything stopped, and a robot helped me out of the armchair. I felt terribly different. I had the impression that everything was simple and easy.

Yahweh spoke again: 'From now on we will see through your eyes, hear through your ears, and speak through your mouth. We will even be able to heal through your hands as we already do at Lourdes and in many other places in the world. We judge that certain sick people deserve our help because of their will to radiate the message we have given you, and because of their efforts to acquire a cosmic mind by opening themselves to infinity.

'We observe everyone. Huge computers ensure a constant surveillance of all people living on Earth. A mark is attributed to everyone depending on whether their actions during their life led towards love and truth or towards hate and obscurantism.

'When the time comes to evaluate, those who went in the right direction will have the right to eternity on this heavenly planet, those who achieved nothing positive yet were not evil will not be recreated, and for those whose actions were particularly negative, a cell from their body will have been preserved, which will allow us to recreate them when the time comes, so that they can be judged and suffer the punishment they deserve.

'You who are reading this message, understand clearly that you can have access to this marvellous world, this paradise. You will be welcome, you who follow our messenger, Claude Raël, our ambassador on the path to universal love and cosmic harmony, you who will help him realise what we will ask of him – for we see through his eyes, hear through his ears, and speak through his mouth.

'Your idea of creating a congregation of guides for humanity is very good. But be strict with regard to their selection so that our message will never be deformed or betrayed.

'Meditation is indispensable for opening one's mind, but asceticism is useless. You must enjoy life with all the strength of your senses, for the awakening of the senses goes together with the awakening of the mind. Continue to play sports if you wish and if you have the time, for all sports and games are good whether they develop musculature or, better still, self-control as do motor racing and motorbike racing.

'A person who feels alone can always try to communicate telepathically with us, while trying to be in harmony with the infinite; he or she will feel an immense sense of well being. What you have advised concerning a gathering of people who believe in us in each region on Sunday mornings at about eleven o'clock is very good. Few members are presently doing this.

'Mediums are useful, so seek them out. But balance them, because their gifts as mediums – which are only gifts of telepathy – unbalance them, and they begin to believe in magic, the supernatural, and other incredibly stupid things, including an ethereal body, which is a new way of trying to believe in the soul which does not exist. In fact, what they are actually doing is tuning into people who lived several centuries ago, and whom we have recreated on this paradisial planet.

'There is an important revelation which you may now make. The Jewish people are our direct descendants on Earth. That is why a specific destiny is reserved for them. They are the descendants of 'the sons of Elohim and the daughters of men' as mentioned in *Genesis*.

'The original mistake of those sons of Elohim was to have mated with their scientific creations, the daughters of human beings. That is why their descendants have suffered for such a long time.

'But for them the time of forgiveness has come, and they will now be able to live peacefully in their recovered country, unless they make another mistake in not recognising you as our messenger. We wish our embassy on Earth to be built in Israel on a tract of land given to you by the government. If they refuse, you may build it elsewhere, and Israel will undergo a new punishment for not having recognised our messenger.

'You must devote yourself entirely to your mission. Do not worry, you will be able to support your family. People who believe in you and therefore in us must help you. You are our messenger, our ambassador, our prophet, and in any case you have your place reserved here among all the other prophets.

'You are the one who must gather together people of all religions. For the movement you have created, the Raëlian Movement, must be the religion of religions. I insist that it is indeed a religion, although an atheistic religion, as you have already understood.

'Those who help you we shall not forget, and those who cause you trouble we shall not forget either. Do not be afraid and fear no one, for whatever happens you have your place amongst us. As for those who lose confidence, shake them up a little.

'Two thousand years ago, those who believed in our messenger Jesus were thrown into a lions' den. Today what do you risk? The irony of fools? The sneers of those who haven't understood anything and prefer to keep to their primitive beliefs? What is all that compared to a lions' den? What is all that compared with what awaits those who follow you? Truly it is easier than ever to follow one's intuition.

'In the Koran, Muhammed, who is among us, has already said on the subject of prophets:

The moment for men to give account is drawing near; and yet in their nonchalance they are turning away (from their creator).
No new warning comes from their creator whom they ignore and laugh at.
And their hearts are amused by it.
Those who do evil comfort themselves secretly by saying:
Is not this man only a mortal as we are?...

It is a jumble of dreams. He made it all up himself. He is a poet
But let him bring a miracle like those who were sent in time past.
Koran, Sura 21: 1–5.

'Even Muhammed had to suffer the sarcasm of some, and Jesus had to
suffer it as well. When he was on the cross, some said: *"If thou be the Son
of God, come down from the cross. (Matthew 27:40.)"*.

'And yet, as you have seen, Jesus is in marvellous shape and will be for
all eternity, as is Muhammed and all those who followed them and
believed in them. On the other hand those who criticised them will be recreated in order to receive their punishment.

'The computers that monitor those people who have no knowledge of
this message are linked to a system that, at the time of death and from a
distance, automatically samples a cell from which they may be recreated if
they deserve it.

'While waiting to build our embassy, create a seminary for the Guides of
the Raëlian Movement near the area where you reside. It is there that you
who are our prophet, the Guide of Guides, will be able to train those
responsible for spreading our message all over the Earth.'

The New Commandments

YAHWEH then said:

'Those who wish to follow you will apply the laws I am now about to
give you.

You will appear at least once in your lifetime before the Guide of
Guides so that he may transmit your cellular plan through manual contact, or have it transmitted by an initiated guide, to the computer that will
take this into account at your life's final hour of judgment.

You will think at least once a day of the Elohim, your Creators.

You will try to radiate the message of the Elohim around you by every
possible means.

You will, at least once a year, give a donation to the Guide of Guides
that is equal to at least one percent of your annual income, in order to
help him devote himself full time to his mission and travel around the
world to spread this message.

You will, at least once a year, invite the Guide of your region into your home, and you will gather at your place people who are interested in hearing him explain the message in all its dimensions.

If the Guide of Guides should disappear, the new Guide of Guides will be the one who has been designated by the former Guide of Guides. The Guide of Guides will be the guardian of the embassy of the Elohim on Earth, and will be able to live there with his family and with the people of his choice.

You, Claude Raël, you are our ambassador on Earth, and the people who believe in you must provide you with the means to accomplish your mission.

You are the last of the prophets before the Judgement, you are the prophet of the religion of religions, the demystifier and the shepherd of shepherds. You are the one whose coming was announced in all the religions by the ancient prophets, our representatives.

You are the one who will bring back the shepherds' flocks before the water is spilled, the one who will bring back to their creators those they have created. Those who have ears may hear, those who have eyes may see. All those who have their eyes open will see that you are the first prophet who can be understood only by scientifically evolved beings. All that you speak of is incomprehensible to primitive peoples.

This is a sign that will be noticed by those whose eyes are open – the sign of the Revelation, the Apocalypse.'

To the People of Israel

YAHWEH moved towards a conclusion by saying:

'The State of Israel must give some territory located near Jerusalem to the Guide of Guides so that he may build there the residence, the embassy of the Elohim. The time has come, people of Israel, to build the new Jerusalem as it was foreseen. Claude Raël is the one who was foretold. Reread your writings and open your eyes.

We wish to have our embassy among our descendants, and the people of Israel are the descendants of the children born of the unions between the sons of Elohim and the daughters of men.

157

People of Israel, we removed you from the clutches of the Egyptians and you did not show yourselves worthy of our confidence; we entrusted you with a message destined for all humanity and you jealously kept it instead of spreading it abroad.

You have suffered for a long time to pay for your errors, but the time of forgiveness has come, and as was foreseen we have said: "To the North give them up and to the South do not hold them back." I have gathered your sons and daughters "from the ends of the Earth," as was written in *Isaiah*, and you have been able to find your country again. You will be able to live there in peace if you listen to the last of the prophets, the one who was foretold to you, and if you help him to accomplish what we ask of him.

This is your last chance, otherwise another country will welcome the Guide of Guides and build our embassy on its territory, and that country will be close to yours; it will be protected and happiness shall prevail, and the State of Israel will be destroyed once more.

You, child of Israel who has not yet returned to your ancestral lands, wait before returning there to see if the government will agree to our embassy being built there. If they refuse, do not return, and you will be one of those who will be saved from the destruction and whose descendants will one day be able to find the promised land again, when the time comes.

People of Israel, recognise the one foretold to you, give him the territory to build our embassy, and help him build it. Otherwise, as happened 2,000 years ago, it will be constructed elsewhere, and if it is constructed elsewhere, you will be dispersed once again. If, 2,000 years ago, you had recognised that Jesus was indeed our messenger, all the Christians in the world would not be Christians, but Jews. You would not have had problems, and you would have remained our ambassadors. But instead this task was given to other people who took Rome for their base.

Two thousand years ago you did not recognise our messenger, and it was not Jerusalem but Rome that shone. Now you have a new chance for it to be Jerusalem once more. If you do not seize it, another country will shelter our embassy and you will no longer have any right to the land we had chosen for you.

There, I have finished. You will be able to annotate all this by yourself once you have returned to Earth. Now enjoy this paradise a while longer, and we will take you back for you to complete your mission before returning to us for good.'

I remained there for several more hours, enjoying the many pleasures of that world, meandering amongst numerous fountains and enjoying the company of the great prophets whom I had met the day before during meditation sessions. Then, after a last meal taken with the same people as the day before, I found myself once again in the large vessel, which set me down at the observation station. From there I retraced my route of the day before, and found myself with my clothes in the small craft which dropped me off where it had picked me up, at Roc Plat. I looked at my watch – it was midnight.

I returned home, where I immediately set to work to write down all that I had been told. Everything was perfectly clear in my mind, and I was surprised to find that I was writing it all at one stroke, recalling without any hesitation the sentences I had heard. The words remained as if engraved in my mind just as I had been told they would at the beginning.

When I finished the account of what had happened, I began to feel very clearly that something had been released inside me. This had never happened before. I began writing again, all the while observing closely what I was putting down as if I was simultaneously discovering it as a reader. I was writing, but this time I did not feel like the author of what was appearing on the paper. The Elohim were starting to speak through my mouth or, rather, to write with my hand.

What was being written before my eyes dealt with all areas that a person is confronted with during his or her lifetime, and the right way to react when faced with these problems. It was, in fact, a code of life – a new way of behaving in the face of life's events, of behaving like an adult, that is to say, as an evolved being, and therefore trying in every way to open one's mind to infinity and to place oneself in harmony with it.

These great rules dictated by the Elohim, our creators, 'Our Fathers who art in Heaven,' as our ancestors used to say without really understanding, are all set forth here in the following pages in their entirety.

3

THE KEYS

Introduction

FOR thousands of years those opposed to enlightenment and reform have effectively imprisoned our minds in straitjackets. These writings, however, are the keys we can use to set ourselves free.

The door to the human mind is fastened by many locks, all of which must be opened at the same time if one wants to be able to approach the infinite. If only one key is used, the other locks will remain fastened, and if they are not all kept open at the same time, then while the second lock is being freed, the first one will close again, preventing the door from opening.

Human society is afraid of what it does not know, and so it is afraid of what lies behind this door – even if it is happiness gained through knowledge of the truth. Therefore, it applies pressure to prevent people from even partly opening this door because society itself prefers to remain in a state of misfortune and ignorance.

This is yet another obstacle found on the threshold of the doorway through which the mind must pass to free itself. But, as Gandhi said: 'It is not because no one sees the truth that it becomes an error.' So if you attempt to open this door, ignore the sarcasm of those who have not seen anything – and of those who having seen, pretend not to see, because of their fear of the unknown.

Also if opening the door seems too difficult for you, ask for help from a guide, since guides have already opened the doors of their own minds and know the difficulties involved. They will not be able to open your door for you, but they will be able to explain the different techniques that will enable you to succeed. Besides, they are living witnesses of the happiness that can be achieved by opening the door, and they prove wrong those who are afraid of what lies behind the door.

Humanity

RIGHT from the start, we must always consider things on four levels.
In relation to infinity.
In relation to the Elohim, our parents and creators.
In relation to human society, and finally:
In relation to the individual.
The most important level is that relating to infinity for it is in relation to this level that all things must be judged – but always with one constant factor: love. This means taking into account those who must be given love, because we must live in harmony with infinity and to do this we must live in harmony with others, because they are a part of infinity as well.

Then we must take into account the advice given by our creators, the Elohim, and act in such a way that human society listens to the advice of those who created it.

Then we must take into account society, which makes it possible for individuals to blossom on the path of truth. But although society must be taken into account, it should not be followed; on the contrary, society must be helped to emerge from its primitive straitjacket by regular questioning of all its habits and traditions, even if these are supported by laws, because laws can also imprison our minds in shackles of obscurantism.

Finally, we must take into account the fulfilment of the individual. Without this the mind does not reach its full potential and it is impossible to harmonise yourself with infinity and become a new person if you are not fulfilled.

Birth

YOU must never impose any religion whatsoever on a child, who is still but a larva, unable to understand what is happening to itself. So you must neither baptise nor circumcise children, nor submit them to any action that they have not themselves accepted. You must wait for them to reach the age of understanding and choice, and if a religion appeals to them at that time, then they should be free to embrace it.

A birth should be a festive occasion, for the Elohim created us in their image to be capable of reproducing ourselves. By creating a living being, we preserve our own species and respect the work of our creators.

A birth should also be an act of love, achieved in harmony as far as sounds, colours and temperature are concerned, so that the human being who is emerging into life develops the habit of being in harmony.

You must immediately develop in children the habit of respecting the liberty of others, and when they cry at night, go to them discreetly but without their realising that crying has brought them the comfort of being tended. On the contrary, you must go to them and look after them when they make no sound and not go to them – at least not with their being aware of it – when they cry. That way they will get used to everything going better when they are in harmony with their surroundings. 'God helps those who help themselves.'

In fact, parents must understand that as soon as a child is born, it is first of all an individual, and that no individual should be treated like a child.

Even our creators do not treat us like children, but as individuals. That is why they do not intervene directly to help us solve our problems but allow us to overcome the obstacles that we encounter by working things out for ourselves as responsible individuals.

Education

THE little creature who is still just the larva of a human being must, in its infancy, grow accustomed to respecting the liberty and the tranquillity of others. Since little children are too young to understand and reason, corporal punishment should be rigorously applied by the person bringing them up, so that they suffer when they cause suffering or disturb others by showing a lack of respect.

This corporal punishment should be applied only to very young children, and then always in keeping with the child's growing power to reason and understand. It should be phased out progressively and eventually be stopped altogether. From the age of seven, corporal punishment should be quite exceptional, and from the age of fourteen, it should never be applied.

You will use corporal punishment only when punishing a child for not respecting the freedom and tranquillity of others or yourself.

You will teach your child to blossom and you will teach him or her always to have a questioning attitude towards those things which society and its schools want to inculcate. You will not force your child to learn things that are not useful, and you will let him or her follow any desired path because, do not forget, the most important thing is his or her fulfilment.

You will teach your child always to judge things in the right order with respect to infinity, with respect to our creators, with respect to society, and with respect to itself.

You will not impose any religion on your child, but instead impartially teach him or her the various beliefs that exist throughout the world – or at least the most important ones in chronological order: – the Jewish religion, the Christian religion and the Muslim religion. You will try to learn the major trends of thought of the Eastern religions, if you can, so that you are able to explain them to your child. Finally, you will explain to him or her the main points of the message given by the Elohim to the last of the prophets.

Above all, you will teach your child to love the world in which it lives and, through this world, our creators.

You will teach him or her to open up to infinity, and try to live in harmony with infinity.

You will teach your child about the marvellous work accomplished by the Elohim, our creators, and constantly seek ways for humanity to become capable of repeating some day what our creators have done – namely creating other humanities elsewhere by scientific means.

You will teach your child to consider itself a part of the infinite – that is, both immense and minute at the same time. 'From dust were ye made, and dust ye shall become.'

You will teach your child that the wrong done to others cannot be undone by any confession or absolution once it is done, and that it must not be thought that when death is near, it is sufficient to begin to believe in the Elohim or any god in order to have the right to eternal life.

You will teach your child that we are judged by what we do throughout our lives, that the path which leads to wisdom is long, and that it certainly

163

takes a whole lifetime to master it sufficiently. A person who has not gone in the right direction throughout life will not gain the right to scientific resurrection on the planet of the eternals just by making a sudden late change to the right path – that is, unless that person's regret is truly genuine and he or she acts with great sincerity, making up for lost time, striving to be forgiven by those who were harmed, and devoting all his or her means to bringing them love and happiness.

All this will still not be enough for the person who has made others suffer, for even if he or she is forgiven by them and gives them love, the errors will have been erased but nothing positive will have been accomplished. This person will then have to set out anew, and bring happiness to new people whom he or she has never harmed, and help those who spread the truth, the guides.

But it is too late for someone who has regrets only at the moment of death or shortly before. This person will not be forgiven.

Sensual Education

SENSUAL education is one of the most important things, and yet at the moment it scarely exists at all.

You will awaken the mind of your child, but you will also awaken his or her body, for the awakening of the body is linked to the awakening of the mind. All those who seek to numb the body are also numbing the mind.

Our creators have given us our senses so we might use them. The nose is meant for smelling, the eyes for seeing, the ears for hearing, the mouth for tasting, and the fingers for touching. We must develop our senses so as to get more enjoyment from all those things which our creators put here for us to enjoy.

A sensual individual is far more likely to be in harmony with infinity, because such a person can feel it without it having to meditate or reflect. However, meditation and reflection will enable that individual to understand this harmony better and to radiate it all around himself or herself by teaching.

To be sensual means to let your environment give you pleasure. Sexual education is very important as well, but it only teaches the technical functions and uses of the organs. Sensual education on the other hand, teaches us how to gain pleasure from our organs purely for pleasure's sake, without necessarily seeking to use them for their utilitarian purposes.

To say nothing to your children about their sexual organs is wrong, and although it is better to explain what they are for, this is still not enough. You must explain how they can gain pleasure from them.

To explain only their function would be like telling them that music is for marching to, that knowing how to write is helpful only for penning letters of complaint, or that movies are useful only for giving audio visual courses, and other such nonsense. Fortunately, thanks to artists and through the awakening of our senses, we can obtain pleasure from listening, reading or looking at works of art that were made for no other reason than to give pleasure. The same goes for the sexual organs. They are not just for satisfying our natural needs or for ensuring reproduction, but also for giving pleasure to ourselves and others. Thanks to science, we have finally emerged from the days when showing one's body was a 'sin', and when sexual intercourse brought its own punishment – the conception of a child.

Now thanks to contraceptive techniques, sexual union is freely possible without it becoming a definitive commitment – or even a possible one. You will teach your child all this without shame but, on the contrary, with love, clearly explaining that he or she was made to be happy and blossom fully – that is to say, to enjoy life with all the senses and with their full force.

You must never be ashamed of your body or of your nakedness, for nothing displeases our creators more than to see those they created feeling ashamed of the appearance that has been given to them.

You will teach your children to love their bodies and every part of the Elohim's creation, because in loving their creation, we love them as well.

Each one of our organs was created by our parents, the Elohim, so that we might use it feeling not shame, but happiness at using something for which it was designed. If the act of using one of our organs brings pleasure, it means that our creators wish us to have that pleasure.

Every individual is a garden that should not be left uncultivated. A life without pleasure is an uncultivated garden. Pleasure is the fertiliser that opens up the mind. Asceticism is useless unless it is a temporary ordeal designed to train the mind to dominate the body. But once we have succeeded in the ordeal that we have set ourselves – which must always be limited in time – we should once more enjoy the pleasures of life.

Asceticism can be accepted as the fallow period of that garden which is an individual – that is to say, a momentary pause in the search for pleasure which enables us to appreciate it better later on.

You will accustom your children to having more and more freedom by always treating them as individuals. You will respect their tastes and inclinations as you would like them to respect your own. Make sure you realise that your child, male or female, is what it is, and that you will not be able to make it what you want, just as it will not be able to make you what it wants you to be. Respect your child so that it respects you, and respect its tastes so that it respects yours.

Fulfilment

SELF FULFILMENT should be sought according to one's tastes and aspirations, without any preoccupation with what others think as long as no one else is being hurt.

If you feel like doing something, first see that it does no harm to anyone, then do it without worrying about what others think of it.

If you feel like having a sensual or sexual experience with one or several other individuals, whatever sex they may be, you may behave as you desire as long as they agree. Everything is permitted on the path to fulfilment in order to awaken the body, and hence the mind.

We are at last emerging from those primitive times when women were seen merely as instruments of reproduction for society. Thanks to science, women are now free to fulfil themselves sensually, without having to fear the punishment of pregnancy. At last, woman is truly the equal of man since she may enjoy her body without living in fear of having to endure alone the undesired consequences of her acts.

Conceiving a child is something too important to be left to chance. Therefore do so only by choice after mature consideration in a marvellous act of love, being fully aware of what you are doing, and being certain that you truly wish it. After all, a child cannot become a successful individual unless it is truly desired at the very moment of conception.

The moment of conception is most important because it is at that time that the first cell, and therefore the plan of the individual, is conceived. This moment must therefore be desired, so that the first cell may be created in perfect harmony, with the minds of the two parents thinking strongly and consciously of the human being that they are conceiving. This is one of the secrets of the new individual.

If you are looking only for the fulfilment of your body, and therefore of your mind, use the means that science has put at your disposal – know from the start about contraception. Only conceive a child when you yourself are fulfilled, so that the life you conceive may be the fruit of the union of two fulfilled individuals.

To reach fulfilment, use the means that science has provided to enable you to awaken your body to pleasure without any risks. Pleasure and procreation are two different things that must not be confused. The first is for the individual and the second is for the species. It is only when the individual is fulfilled that he or she can create a fulfilled human being.

If by accident you have conceived a child without desiring it, use the means that science puts at your disposal – abortion. A child who was not desired at the moment of conception cannot blossom fully since it was not created in harmony. Do not listen to those who try to frighten you by talking about the physical – and especially ethical – consequences that an abortion can trigger. There are none if you are treated by competent people. Keeping an undesired child, however, can leave you with physical and moral disturbances that can be passed on, making the child you brought into the world suffer too.

Having a child does not necessarily imply that you must be married or even live with a man. Already, many women have decided to have one or more children without marrying or living with a man. The education of a child, who is an individual right from birth, should not necessarily be provided by the parents. It would indeed often be preferable for education to be entrusted to specialised people who would contribute far more than some parents towards their children's fulfilment.

If you wish to have a child without living with a man, do as you desire. Fulfil yourself as you would like, without worrying what others think.

If you choose to do this, do not think that you are condemned to live alone forever. Welcome the men you like, and they will serve as masculine role models for your child.

You can even decide one day to live with a man – this will not cause any problems for your child at all. On the contrary, it will contribute to his or her fulfilment. A change of environment is always positive for a child.

Society should organise itself to take charge of the education of children partially or totally, depending on the parents' wishes. Those parents who want to work should be able to leave their children in the custody of competent people, and those who want their children to receive an education given entirely by such individuals should be able to entrust their children completely to establishments created for this purpose. In this way, if you give birth to a child you desired, but afterwards you separate from your companion, or for any other reason you no longer desire the child, you will be able to entrust your child to society, so that it may be brought up surrounded by the harmony necessary for its fulfilment. A child who grows up in surroundings where it is not really and truly wanted cannot blossom and be fulfilled.

Bringing up a child should be mutually fulfilling for both parent and offspring. If a child becomes a nuisance, however slight, it realises this and fulfilment is affected. A child should therefore be kept near you only if its presence is felt to be fulfilling.

Otherwise the child should be put in establishments that society must create to encourage fulfilment, and be placed there without the least regret. On the contrary, parents should feel a profound sense of joy because they are entrusting their child to others more capable than themselves of helping each little individual to blossom.

Regular visits can even take place if the children, whose wishes are of primary importance, would like them. The people in charge of the children's education should always describe the parents as exceptional people, who placed more importance on their children's fulfilment than on their own selfish pleasure of bringing them up themselves. They did this, the children should be told, by entrusting them to people more competent than themselves.

Choose your partner freely if you desire one. Marriage, whether religious or civil, is useless. You cannot sign a contract to unite living individuals, who are bound to change because they are alive.

Reject marriage which is only the public proclamation of ownership of a person. A man or woman cannot be the property of anyone else. Any contract can only destroy the harmony existing between two individuals.

When we feel loved, we feel free to love, but when we have signed a contract, we feel like prisoners who are forced to love each other, and sooner or later we begin to hate each other. So you will live with the person of your choice only for as long as you feel happy with him or her.

When you no longer get on well together, do not remain together, because your union will become hell. All living beings evolve, and rightly so. If the personal evolution of each individual is similar, the union lasts but if their progress is different, then union is no longer possible. You no longer like the individual you used to like, because one of you has changed. You must part from each other while retaining happy memories of your time together, instead of spoiling it with useless bickering which gives way to hostility. A child chooses clothes that fit, and when it outgrows them they must be changed for different clothes, otherwise they will be torn to pieces.

Above all, do not be worried about your child. It is better for him or her to be with only one parent in harmony than to be with both in discord, or lacking perfect harmony. Do not forget that children are, above all, individuals.

Society must make absolutely sure that old people have a happy life without any material worries. But although we must respect the aged and do everything to make them happy we should not listen to them just because of their seniority.

An intelligent person can give good advice at any age, but a stupid person, even if he is a hundred years old, does not deserve to be listened to for a second. What is more, such a person has no excuse, having had an entire lifetime in which to try to awaken, whereas there is still hope for a young and stupid person. But in any case, a stupid old person must still be able to live comfortably. This is a duty for society.

Death should not be an occasion for sad gatherings; on the contrary, it should be a time of joyful celebration, because it is the moment when the beloved one may perhaps reach the paradise of the eternals in the company of our creators, the Elohim.

You will therefore ask not to be buried religiously, but you will donate your body to science or you will ask that your body be disposed of as discreetly as possible, except for the bone of your forehead – more precisely the part located above the beginning of the nose 33 millimetres (1.3 inches) above the middle of the axis linking the pupils of your eyes. At least one square centimetre (0.4 square inches) of this bone should be sent to the Guide of Guides so that he may keep it in our embassy on Earth.

Each person is monitored by a computer that records all their actions and makes a tally of them at the end of their life. But people who know about this message which Claude Raël is communicating will be re-created from the cells that they have left in our embassy. In their cases re-creation will take place only if they ensure that the required part of their body is sent to the Guide of Guides after their death.

The mechanism within the computer that records the information to be used in judgement of individuals remains in operation after they learn about the message. But the mechanism that allows an automatic sampling of a cell at the moment of death is disconnected. So only those who comply exactly with what is required once they know about the message will be recreated.

Make sure that at least once in your life you see the Guide of Guides or a guide authorised by him to transmit your cellular plan to the Elohim, so that they may awaken your mind and help you to remain awakened.

In accordance with what is written earlier in this message you will not leave an inheritance to your children, except for the family house or apartment. The rest you will leave in your will to the Guide of Guides, and if you fear your descendants might not respect your last will and testament but might try to recover your property through the courts, you will bestow it while you are alive on the Guide of Guides, in order to help him spread the message of our creators on Earth.

Those of you who remain after the death of a loved one, do not be sad and lament. Try instead to give love to those you love while they are still living, because once they are dead, what makes you unhappy is the thought that perhaps you did not love them enough, and that now it is too late.

Anyone who was good in their lifetime has the right to the Elohim's gardens for eternity and will know happiness, and anyone who was not good does not deserve to be missed.

But even if an individual is not among those chosen for re-creation, he or she does not really vanish. Death is not a very important thing, and we should not be afraid of it. It is just like falling asleep, except it is an endless sleep. Since we are a part of infinity, the matter of which we are made does not disappear. It continues to exist in the soil, or in plants, or even in animals, clearly losing all homogeneity and, therefore, all identity. This part of infinity that was organised by our creators according to a very precise structure, returns to infinity while remaining a part of this small ball called the Earth, which is alive.

Everyone has the right to live, the right to love and the right to die. Everyone is the director of his or her own life and death. Death is nothing, but suffering is terrible, and everything must be done to eliminate it. Someone who is suffering too much has the right to commit suicide. If this person's actions were positive during his or her life, he or she will be admitted to the planet of the eternals.

If someone you love suffers very much and wishes to die, but does not have the strength to commit suicide, help them to take their own life.

When science one day enables you to eliminate human suffering, then you can ask yourselves whether it is right to commit suicide or not.

Society and Government

JUST as a human body has a brain, it is essential that society should have a government to make decisions. So you will do everything you can to set up a government that practises geniocracy, which puts intelligence in power. You will also participate in the creation of a worldwide political party advocating humanitarianism and geniocracy, as they are described in the first part of this message of the Elohim, and you will support its candidates. Only via geniocracy can humanity move fully into the golden age.

Total democracy is not good. A body in which all the cells command cannot survive. Only intelligent people should be permitted to make decisions involving humanity. You will therefore refuse to vote, unless a candidate advocating geniocracy and humanitarianism is standing for election.

Neither universal suffrage nor public opinion polls are valid ways of governing the world. To govern is to foresee, not to follow the reactions of a sheep-like population, among whom only a very small number are sufficiently awakened to guide humanity. Since there are very few awakened people, if we base decisions on universal suffrage or opinion polls, the decisions become the choice of the majority – and therefore of those who are not awakened. Such people respond in the interests of their immediate gratification, or as a result of instinctive reactions which are unconsciously confined in a straitjacket of obscurantist conditioning.

Only geniocracy, which is a selective democracy, is worthwhile. As was stated in the first part of this message of the Elohim, only people whose net level of intelligence is fifty per cent above average should be eligible to stand for election and only those whose net level of intelligence is ten per cent above the average should be eligible to vote. Scientists are already developing techniques to measure net intelligence. Follow their advice, and act in such a way that the most precious mineral of humanity – exceptionally gifted children – may receive an education at a level appropriate to their genius, since normal education is designed only for children of average intelligence.

It is not the number of diplomas that one has obtained that signifies intelligence since this only calls upon the rather uninteresting faculty of memory, which machines can replace. Intelligence in its raw state is the quality that can make peasants or workers much more intelligent than engineers or professors. This can be spoken of as common sense, as well as creative genius, because most inventions are nothing more than a matter of common sense.

As already stated, to govern is to foresee, and all the great problems that humanity is now facing prove that past governments did not have foresight and were therefore incompetent governments. The problem does not lie with the people who govern but rather the technique that is used to choose them: the problem is the way we select those who govern us. Basic democracy must be replaced by a selective democracy – that is geniocracy, which puts intelligent people in power. This is a very fundamental requirement.

Human laws are indispensable, and you will respect them, while seeing to it that those that are unfair or obsolete are changed. However, do not hesitate to choose the laws of our creators above human laws because even human judges will be judged some day by our creators.

The police will be essential for as long as it takes society to discover the medical means to eradicate violence and prevent criminals or those who infringe the freedom of others from acting out their antisocial impulses. Unlike soldiers, who are the keepers of war, police officers are the keepers of peace and they will remain indispensable until science has solved this problem.

In countries where compulsory military service exists you will refuse to participate. Instead ask to be granted the status of a conscientious objector, which will allow you to serve in a division that does not carry weapons, as is your right if your religious or philosophical convictions forbid you to kill your fellow human beings. This is the case for those who believe in the Elohim, our creators, and want to follow the directives of the Guide of Guides of the Raëlian Movement.

Contrary to what many young people think, conscientious objectors are not sent to jail, but serve instead in some civilian role or in an unarmed division for a period that is double the normal duration of military service. It is better to spend two years working in an office than to be trained for one year in techniques that enable you to kill fellow human beings.

Military service must be eliminated immediately in all the countries of the world. All professional soldiers must be transformed into guardians of world peace who work in the service of freedom and human rights.

The only system of government that is worthwhile is geniocracy applying humanitarianism. Capitalism is wrong because it enslaves people to money, benefiting a few on the backs of others. Communism is also wrong, since it places greater importance on equality than on liberty. There must be equality among people at the beginning, at birth, but not afterwards. Although everyone has the right to have sufficient means to live decently, those who do more for their fellow human beings have the right to receive more than those who do nothing for the community.

This is obviously a temporary rule until all menial labour can be performed by robots. Then, after totally abolishing money, all people may devote themselves exclusively to their own personal fulfilment. In the meantime it is shameful that while some people are dying of hunger, others throw food away to prevent prices collapsing. Instead of throwing away this food, they should distribute it to those who have nothing to eat.

Work must not be considered sacred. Everyone has the right to live comfortably, even if they do not work, and should try to fulfil themselves and blossom in whatever field attracts them. If people are organised, it will not take them long to mechanise and automate all indispensable work. Then everybody will be able to grow freely and achieve a sense of fulfilment.

If all individuals really set their minds to it, in only a few years freedom from the need to work could be attained. What is required is a marvellous burst of enthusiasm and solidarity in working for the liberation of humankind from material constraints.

All humanity's technical and scientific resources should be pooled and all those working in these areas should truly set their minds on striving together for the well-being of the entire community, rather than for vested interests. Use all the resources which are currently wasted on military budgets or the inane development of nuclear weapons – or even flights into space. Such things could be better planned and much more easily accomplished once humanity is free of material constraints.

You have computers and electronic equipment that can better replace manpower. Put them all to work so that this technology can truly operate in the service of humankind. In a few years you can build a completely different world. You have reached the golden age.

Do everything possible to create the biological robot that will release you from all menial labour and enable you to blossom and fulfil yourselves.

Urban development must be reconsidered as it is described in the first part of this message of the Elohim. You must build very tall communal houses situated in open country, so that individual houses do not 'devour' nature. Never forget that if everyone had a country house with a small garden, there would be no more countryside. These communal houses must be cities that are equipped with everything people need, and be capable of accommodating about 50,000 inhabitants each.

Until the day you become creators and can re-create it yourselves, you must respect nature. By respecting nature, you respect those who created it – our parents, the Elohim.

You will never make animals suffer. You may kill them to feed on their flesh, but do this without making them suffer. Although as already indicated, death is nothing, suffering is an abomination, and you must avoid making animals suffer as you must prevent human beings from suffering.

Nevertheless, do not eat too much meat, and you will feel better for it. You may live on all that the land provides. You do not have to follow a special diet; you may eat meat, vegetables, fruits and other plants. But it is foolish to follow a vegetarian diet under the pretext that you do not want to live on the meat of other living creatures. Plants are alive just as you are, and suffer in the same way that you do. So you must not cause suffering to plants.

Do not intoxicate yourself with alcoholic beverages. You may drink a little wine while eating, for it is a product of the earth. But never intoxicate yourself. You may drink alcoholic beverages in exceptional circumstances, but in very small quantities and accompanied by solid food so that you never get drunk. Anyone who is drunk is no longer capable of being in harmony with infinity, nor able to control themselves. This is something appalling in the eyes of our creators.

You will not smoke, for the human body was not made to inhale smoke. This has appalling effects on the organism, and prevents total fulfilment and harmonisation with infinity.

You will not take drugs. You will not drug yourself in any way, for the awakened mind needs nothing outside itself to approach infinity. It is an abomination in the eyes of our creators that people think they must take drugs to improve themselves. Human beings have no need to improve themselves because all are perfect, having been made in the image of our creators.

To say that a human being is imperfect is to insult our creators who made us in their image. But although we are perfect, we cease to be so if we think of ourselves as imperfect and remain resigned to such thoughts. To remain perfect as we were created by the Elohim, we need to make an effort at every moment of the day to keep ourselves in an awakened state.

Meditation and Prayer

YOU should meditate at least once each day locating yourself in relation to infinity, in relation to the Elohim, to society, and yourself. You should meditate upon awakening so that your whole being becomes fully conscious of infinity and you are placed in full possession of all your faculties.

You should meditate before each meal, so that all parts of your body eat when you eat; and when you nourish yourself, think of what you are doing.

Your meditation will not be a dry meditation, but on the contrary, a sensual meditation. You will let yourself be engulfed by peace and harmony until it becomes a pleasurable delight. Your meditation should not be forced labour, but a pleasure. It is better not to meditate at all than to meditate without really wanting to do so.

Do not impose meditation on your children or your family. But explain to them the pleasure that it gives and the sense of well-being that it brings, and if they then feel like meditating, try to teach them what you know.

Think intensely of the Elohim, our creators, at least once a day, and try to communicate with them telepathically. In this way you will rediscover the original meaning of prayer. If you do not know how to go about it, you can take your inspiration from the Lord's Prayer, the words of which are perfectly appropriate for communication with our creators.

At least once a week attempt group telepathic communication with the Elohim alongside other people from your region who believe in them. If possible you should be accompanied by a Guide.

Do your very best every year to attend the meeting of all those who believe in the Elohim and in the message they have given to the last of the prophets.

Technique for Attempting Telepathic Contact with the Elohim

HERE is a model of what you could say while looking towards the sky and thinking intensely about the words.

Elohim, you are there somewhere near those stars.

Elohim, you are there, and I know you are watching us.

Elohim, you are there, and I would so much like to meet you.

Elohim, you are there, and who am I to hope to deserve a contact?

Elohim, I recognise you as our creators, and I place myself humbly at your service.

Elohim, I recognise Claude Raël, your messenger, as my guide, and I believe in him and in the message you gave him.

Elohim, I will do my best to make the message known to those around me, because I know I have not done enough.

Elohim, I love all human beings as my brothers and sisters because they are made in your image.

Elohim, I am trying to bring them happiness by opening their minds to infinity and revealing to them what was revealed to me.

Elohim, I am trying to stop their suffering by placing my whole being at the service of humankind, of which I am a part.

Elohim, I am trying to use to the utmost the mind you have given me, to help humankind emerge from darkness and suffering.

Elohim, I hope that you will judge the little I have done by the end of my life to be sufficient to grant me the right to eternal life on the planet of the wise.

I love you, as you must have loved human beings to admit the best of them among your eternals.

The Arts

DO your best to encourage artists, and to help your child if he or she is attracted by the arts. Art is one of the things which best enables you to harmonise with infinity. Consider every natural thing an art, and every art a natural thing. Surround yourself with artistic things, whether they appeal to your ears, your eyes, your sense of touch, smell or taste.

Everything which appeals to the senses is artistic. There is more than just music, painting, sculpture and all the officially recognised arts. Gastronomy is also an art, as well as perfume-making, since they both appeal to the senses. Standing above all finally, love is an art.

All art makes use of harmony, and therefore allows those who appreciate it to be taken over by something harmonious. This consequently produces the right conditions for placing oneself in harmony with infinity.

Literature is particularly important because it contributes to opening people's minds by showing them new horizons. But literature for literature's sake is just prattle; what counts is not writing beautiful sentences, but the transmission of new ideas to others through reading.

Audio visual means are even more important, for they appeal to our senses of sight and hearing at the same time. They could well replace literature, since they are more complete. Meanwhile, literature is useful for the time being.

Sensual Meditation

IF you want to reach a high level of harmony with infinity, arrange a place of sensual meditation for yourself. Place in it works of art, paintings, reproductions, tapestries, posters, sculptures, drawings, photographs or anything else that is intended to represent love, infinity and sensuality for the enjoyment of your eyes.

Arrange for yourself a corner where you can sit close to the ground, on cushions, for example. Or lie down on a couch or on fur, for the pleasure of touching it. Evaporate agreeable scents and oils to please your nose. Have a tape recorder and a cassette on which you have recorded music that you like for the pleasure of your ears.

Have trays and bottles filled with food and drink that you like for the pleasure of your mouth, and invite one or several people you love, who share your tastes and with whom you feel at ease and in harmony; then feed your senses together and open your bodies in order to open your minds in love and fraternity.

If someone appeals to you physically and you feel that it is reciprocal, invite him or her to this place. Together you can reach a sublime state of harmony, which will enable you to approach infinity by satisfying your five senses. To this state will be added the synthesis of all these enjoyments – the physical union of two individuals in total harmony and in the illumination of the act of love.

Obviously, the harmony must first exist spiritually. In other words, there must be a mutual attraction between *the minds and the bodies* of the individuals in the way they approach and respect each other. But a spiritual love is always made sublime by a fulfilled physical love. To love is to give and expect nothing in exchange. If you love somebody, you should give yourself to this person entirely if he or she desires it.

Never be jealous, for jealousy is the opposite emotion to love. When you love someone, you must seek his or her happiness first and foremost, and in every way. To love is to seek the happiness of others, and not your own. If the person you love is attracted to another, do not be jealous; on the contrary, be happy that the one you love is happy, even if it is because of somebody else.

Love also the person who, like you, wants to bring happiness to the person you love, and who therefore has the same goal as you. Jealousy is the fear that someone else may make the person you love happier than you do yourself, and that you may lose the one you love. But instead of feeling jealous we should try to do as much as possible to make the person we love happy, and if somebody else succeeds better in this, we should be happy about it. What counts is not that our beloved be happy because of us but simply that they be happy, whoever is responsible.

So if the person you love is happy with somebody else, rejoice in this happiness. You will recognise the person who loves you in that he or she will not oppose your happiness with someone else.

It is your duty to love the person who loves you that much and to give him or her happiness yourself. In that direction lies the path of universal love.

Do not reject someone who wants to make you happy, for by accepting them you make them happy, and this is an act of love. Rejoice in the happiness of others, so that they may rejoice in yours.

Human Justice

HUMAN laws, as already stated, are essential. But they must be improved upon because they do not take love and fraternity sufficiently into consideration.

The death penalty must be abolished because no individual has the right to kill another coldly in a premeditated, organised manner. Until the time comes when, through science, society is able to control the violence that occurs in some people and can cure them of their illness, you will keep criminals apart from society. Then give them the love that they have lacked, while trying to make them understand the monstrous nature of their actions. Give them also the desire to redeem themselves.

Do not mix hardened criminals – who are suffering from an illness that can be contagious – with people who have merely committed petty offences. That way you will avoid contaminating the lesser offenders.

Never forget that all criminals are sick, and always consider them as such. We are shocked when we remember that once upon a time we used to suffocate people between mattresses if they suffered from fits of hysteria. Some day when we are able to cure and, more importantly, prevent, the sickness of crime, we will be just as shocked when we look back at how we used to execute criminals.

Forgive those who have done you harm unintentionally and bear no grudge against those who have willingly done you harm. They are ill, for one must be ill to harm one's neighbour. Besides, think how unfortunate those people are, who do harm others, because they will not have the right to eternal life in the gardens of the Elohim.

But if someone wants to harm you or those you love, try to subdue them. If you cannot, then you have the right to defend yourself to save your own life or the lives of your loved ones. However, never strike with the intention to kill, even in legitimate defence. Try only to render the person harmless – by knocking him or her out, for example. If the blow you give turns out to be fatal, you have nothing to blame yourself for, as long as you did not have the intention to kill.

You will subdue violent people by force, and, if necessary, by direct action. Violent behaviour is intolerable, and you will not tolerate it, even if you have to forcibly restrain violent people. But always use a non-violent force, that is to say, a balanced force applied without malicious intent, sufficient only to overcome those who try to do harm.

Any threat of violence should be treated as seriously as an actual violent deed. To threaten violence is to think it possible, and to see it as an acceptable way of achieving one's goals. A person capable of threatening another with violence is as dangerous as someone who has already committed a violent act. Until we can find a medical cure for those who make such threats, they must be kept outside society, and we must try to make them understand that their behaviour is dreadful.

When dealing with those who take hostages, think first of the lives of innocent people who are not in the hands of the hostage-takers. People who take hostages are sick and you should not give them what they demand. Society in fact must never give in to them because by doing so you encourage other criminals to copy such actions and give credence to their threats.

All human beings must have equal rights and opportunities at birth, whatever race they may be. Discriminate against fools, however, whatever the colour of their skin. All the races that populate the Earth were created by the Elohim, and must be equally respected.

Humanity as a whole must unite to form a world government, as it is written in the first part of this message. Impose also a new world language on all the schoolchildren of the entire world. Esperanto exists, and if no one proposes anything better, choose Esperanto.

Until it becomes possible to abolish money, create a new world currency to replace national currencies. Therein lies the solution to the monetary crisis. If no one can propose anything better, use the federalist system. Create a federation from all the countries of the world. Grant independence to those regions which need to be able to organise themselves as they wish. The world will live in harmony when it is no longer composed of separate countries, but consists instead of regions united in a federation to take charge of the future of the Earth.

Science

SCIENCE is the most important thing of all for humanity. You will keep yourself in touch with the advances made by scientists, because they can solve all your problems. Do not let scientific discoveries fall into the hands of those who think only of making profit, nor into the hands of the military, who keep certain inventions secret in order to retain a hypothetical supremacy over illusory enemies.

Science should be your religion, for the Elohim created you scientifically. By being scientific, you please your creators, because you are acting as they do, and you show them that you understand that you were made in their image, and are anxious to take advantage of all the potential that you have within you. Science must be used to serve and liberate humankind, not to destroy and alienate it. Trust those scientists who are not being manipulated by financial interests, and only them.

You may participate in sports for they are very good for your equilibrium – particularly those sports that develop self-control. Society should also authorise violent and even very violent sports. These are safety valves. An evolved and non-violent society must have violent games that maintain an image of violence, enabling young people who wish it, to be violent with others who wish the same thing. This also allows others to watch these violent exhibitions and so release their aggressive energies.

You may participate in games that require thought and use of the mind. But as long as money has not been abolished, never play to win money; rather play for the pleasure of making your mind function.

You will date your writings counting the year 1946 as 'year one', after Claude Raël, the last of the prophets. Then 1976 is therefore year 31 after

Claude Raël, or year 31 of the era of Aquarius, or year 31 of the age of the Apocalypse, or year 31 of the golden age.

The Human Brain

WE still have a long way to go in fully understanding the potential of the human brain. For example, the sixth sense, direct perception, should be developed in young children. This is what we call telepathy. Telepathy enables us to communicate directly with our creators, the Elohim.

Numerous mediums have come to me asking what they should do, because they had received messages from what they call 'the beyond' asking them to get in touch with me in order to help me, and for me in my turn to bring them light. Mediums are very important people because they have an above average gift of telepathy and their minds are already on the path to an awakened state. They should try to practise meditation in order to fully master their potential.

I, Claude Raël, am eagerly waiting for all those mediums who have received such messages to get in touch with me, so that we may organise regular meetings. The true mediums who seek to be informed will all receive instructions. The power of one brain is great, but the power of several brains is infinite. Let those who have ears, hear.

Never forget that all those things which you do not understand and which scientists cannot explain have been created by the Elohim. The clockmaker knows all the parts of the clock he has made.

The Apocalypse

DO not forget that the Apocalypse – literally the 'age of revelation' – has arrived as was predicted. It has been said that when the time comes, there will be many false prophets. You only have to look around you to see that the time has indeed come. False prophets are writers of horoscopes, of which the newspapers are full, and there are also many others who reject the benefits of science and cling to every last letter of ancient writings that were the messages given by the Elohim to the primitive people of ancient times.

Such false prophets prefer to believe what narrow-minded and primitive people have fearfully copied down long ago, while listening to those whom they considered to be gods because they came from the sky. They should instead believe the message of the Elohim that has been given now to people who no longer kneel stupidly before all that comes from the sky. These latter people try to understand the universe and they can be addressed as adults. But if you look around, you will see the crowds of fanatic and obscurantist religious sects, which attract young impressionable people thirsty for the truth.

A philosopher once said: 'Jesus came to show people the path to follow, and everybody kept staring at his finger'. Meditate on this sentence. It is not the messenger who matters, but the person who sends the message, and the message itself.

Do not go astray among the sects of the East – the truth is not on top of the Himalayas any more than in Peru or elsewhere. The truth is within you. But if you want to travel and you like exotic places, go to all these distant countries. You will understand then that you have wasted your time, and that what you were looking for was inside you all the time.

Travel within yourself, otherwise you are only a tourist – someone who passes by and thinks he or she will find the truth by watching others search for it within themselves. They may find it, perhaps, but those watching them certainly will not. To travel inside yourself, you do not need to take a plane.

The East has nothing to teach the West about wisdom and awakening the mind. Rather, the opposite is true. How can you find wisdom amongst people who die from hunger as they watch herds of sacred cows go by?

On the contrary, it is the West with its intellect and its science, that comes to help people who for ages have been shackled by primitive and murderous beliefs. It is not by chance that countries in the West no longer face the same problems as those of the Third World. Where the mind rules, the body does not die of hunger. Where obscurantism prevails, the body cannot survive. Can primitive people solve the problems of famine in the world and give food to those who are starving? They already have enough difficulties trying to feed themselves, and you expect to find wisdom there?

All the people of the Earth had the same chances at the beginning. Some have solved their problems, and even have more than they need, while others simply do not have the means to survive. In your opinion, which ones can help the others? The people of the West still have an enormous distance to go on the path of open-mindedness, but the people of the East have not achieved one tenth of what the people of the West have achieved.

Telepathic Communication

'MIND and matter are eternally the same thing' it is stated in the *Bardo Thodol*. the Tibetan *Book of the Dead* and that quotation is an appropriate introduction to this section.

If you want to have telepathic communication of a very high quality, do not cut your hair or your beard. Certain people have a telepathic organ that is sufficiently developed to work well even if their head is shaved. But if you want to achieve the best results, then do not cut what the creators have made grow on your head and face. If it grows, there is a reason, for none of your physical characteristics were given to you without reason. By respecting the creation, you respect the creator.

The best moment to enter into communication with your creators is on waking, because as your body is emerging from sleep your mind is reawakening too. A mechanism starts up at that point, a mechanism which you must activate by deliberately opening your mind as far as possible to everything around you and to infinity. You should take special care not to halt the process.

Sit down cross legged, or better still, lie on your back on the ground. If possible position yourself in the open air and look up towards the sky.

The mind is like a rose. In the morning, it begins to open, but you often prune it when it is still just a bud. If you would wait a little, it would bloom. To practise physical fitness is good, but to practise the physical fitness of the mind is better.

Yet do not be impatient if you do not obtain results right away. When an organ is not used, it atrophies. When you have had a limb in plaster for a long time, you need a lot of physical therapy to recover its normal use.

Look up to the sky and think of your position in the context of everything that surrounds you. Visualise yourself in relation to the house that you occupy, a tiny speck lost between stone walls. See yourself in relation to all the people who are waking up at the same time as you, and in relation to those who, in other parts of the globe, are going to bed. Think of all those who are being born, those who are uniting with each other physically, those who are suffering, working or dying at that time. Think of them all and situate yourself accordingly at your own level of existence.

Situate yourself in relation to the infinitely large as well. Think of the town where you are, a tiny speck lost in a landscape that is the country, the continent or the island where you live. Then fly away in your mind, as if you were in a plane travelling further and further away from the ground, until the town and then the continent are nothing but a tiny spot on the map.

Be aware of the fact that you are on the Earth, a small ball where humanity is but a parasite. It is always spinning although you do not realise this is happening. Situate yourself in relation to it, and in relation to the moon, which is revolving around the Earth, and in relation to the Earth, which is revolving around the sun, and in relation to the sun, which is itself rotating as it revolves around the centre of our galaxy. Situate yourself in relation to the stars that are also suns which have planets orbiting them. On these planets an infinite number of other beings live and among them is the planet of our creators, the Elohim, as well as the planet of the eternals, where you may one day be admitted for eternity.

Locate yourself in relation to all those worlds where other living beings live – some more advanced and some more primitive than we are, and in relation to those galaxies which themselves revolve around the centre of the universe. Finally situate yourself in relation to our whole universe, which itself is an atom of an atom of a molecule located perhaps in the arm of somebody who is looking up at the sky, wondering whether there is life on other planets . . .

This is all in relation to the infinitely large.

Then situate yourself also in relation to your body, to all its vital organs and the other parts of which it is made up. Think of all those organs that are working without your noticing it, right at this very moment.

Think of your heart, which is beating without your asking it to, your blood, which circulates and irrigates your whole body, and your brain, which enables you to reflect and be conscious of doing so. Think of all the corpuscles that make up your blood and of all the cells that are being born in your body, those feeling pleasure while reproducing and those that are dying without your knowing it, and perhaps without being conscious that they help form the individual that you are.

Think too of all the molecules that constitute these cells, and the atoms that constitute these molecules, revolving like suns around the centre of a galaxy, and of the particles that make up these atoms, and of the particles of these particles on which there is life asking itself if there is life on other planets. . .

This is all in relation to the infinitely small.

Place yourself in harmony with the infinitely large and with the infinitely small by radiating love towards what is above and towards what is below, and by being conscious that you yourself are part of infinity. Then by thinking intensely about your message of love to the Elohim, our creators, try to transmit to them your wish to see them, to join them one day, to have the strength to earn the reward of being among the chosen ones. Then you will feel light and ready to do good around you with all your strength all day long, because you will be in harmony with infinity.

You may also do these exercises in the sensual meditation room during the day, alone or with other people. But the moment when you come closest to perfect harmony will occur when this takes place in your room of sensual meditation with someone you love and you unite yourself physically with him or her, and jointly harmonise yourselves with infinity during your union.

In the evening, when the sky is full of stars and the temperature is mild, lie down on the ground. Look up at the heavens, and think intensely of the Elohim, wishing that some day you may deserve to be amongst them, and thinking strongly that you are available and ready to do exactly what they may ask of you, even if you do not clearly understand why they are asking it. Perhaps you will see a signal if you are sufficiently ready.

As you are lying there on your back, be aware of the extent to which your organs of perception are limited, which explains the difficulty you may have in conceiving of infinity. A force keeps you nailed to the ground, you cannot fly off to the stars with a jerk, and yet you do not see any rope holding you down.

Millions of people are listening to thousands of radio stations and watching hundreds of television programmes that are being broadcast in the atmosphere – yet you do not see these waves of sound and vision and you

186

do not hear them. Compasses all have their points drawn to the north, and yet you neither see nor hear the forces that act on them.

So I repeat again – your organs of perception are very limited, and energies like the universe are infinite. Wake yourself up, and wake up the organs you have within you which will allow you to receive waves that you are not yet picking up or do not even suspect. Simple pigeons are able to find the north and you, a human being, cannot. Think about this for a moment.

Furthermore, teach your children, whose organs are developing, all about this. This is how the 'new humanity' will be born, and their faculties will be infinitely superior to those of present human beings.

When his growth is finished, a man who has never learned to walk will always be a cripple, and even if he is taught later, he will always be handicapped, even if he is very gifted. Therefore it is during their growth that you must open the minds of your children, so that all their faculties may blossom, and they will turn into individuals who have nothing in common with what we are: poor, narrow-minded, primitive people.

The Reward

MAY this book guide those who recognise and love our creators, the Elohim. May it guide those who believe in them and those who remember to communicate telepathically with them, thus rediscovering the original meaning of prayer. May it guide those who do good to their fellow human beings. May it guide those who believe in what was revealed to me and in what was revealed before me, and those who are sure that scientific reincarnation is a reality. All such people have a guide and an aim in life, and are happy.

As for those who are not awakened, it is useless to speak to them about this message of the Elohim. One who is asleep cannot hear, and the unconscious mind does not wake up in just a few moments – especially if the person sleeping finds his or her sleep very comfortable.

Spread this message around you to those who do good to their fellow human beings. Spread it particularly among those who, by using the mind that the Elohim gave them, are relieving society from fear of food shortages, disease and the burden of daily exertions. They do this by giving others time to fulfil themselves and blossom and it is for such individuals that the fountained gardens of the planet of the eternals are reserved.

For it is not enough merely to avoid harming others without doing them any good. Anyone whose life has been neutral will be entitled to neutrality. That is to say, he or she will not be re-created, neither to pay for crimes which have not been committed, nor to receive the reward for non-existent good deeds.

Anyone who has made many people suffer during part of his or her life, and then makes up for it by doing as much good as harm, will also be neutral. To have the right to scientific reincarnation on the planet of the eternals, one must have an unambiguously positive assessment at the end of one's life.

To be satisfied with doing good on a small scale around oneself is enough for someone who is not of superior intelligence, or who is not wealthy, but it is not enough for someone who is very intelligent or wealthy. A very intelligent person has a duty to use the mind given to them by the Elohim to bring happiness to others by inventing new techniques to improve their living conditions.

Those people who will be entitled to scientific reincarnation on the planet of the eternals will live in a world where food will be brought to them without their having to make the slightest effort, and where there will be marvellously beautiful female and male partners scientifically created for the sole purpose of satisfying their pleasures. They will live there eternally, seeking only to fulfil themselves doing whatever pleases them. As for those who have made others suffer, they will be recreated, and their suffering will be equal to the pleasure of the eternals.

How can you not believe in all this now that science and ancient religions are coming together perfectly? You were nothing but matter, mere dust, yet the Elohim made you into living beings in their image capable of dominating matter. Later you will again become matter or dust, and they will make you live once more as they have created you, scientifically.

The Elohim created the first human beings without knowing that they were doing what had already been done for them. They thought they were only conducting a minor scientific experiment, and that is why they destroyed almost all of humanity the first time.

But when they understood that they had been created just like us, they began to love us as their own children, and swore never to try to destroy us again, leaving us to overcome our own violence by ourselves.

Although the Elohim do not directly intervene for or against humanity as a whole, they do, however, exert influence on some individuals whose actions please or displease them. Woe to those claiming to have met the Elohim or to have received a message from them if it is not true. Their life will become hell, and they will regret their lie when faced with all the troubles they will encounter.

Also those who act against the Guide of Guides and try to prevent him carrying out his mission, or who go along with him in order to spread strife amongst those who follow him, they will also see their life become hell. Without any obvious influence coming from above, they will know why disease, family and professional difficulties, emotional woes and other problems will all invade their earthly existence while they await their eternal punishment.

You who smile as you read these lines, you are among those who would have crucified Jesus if you had lived in his time. Yet now you want to see members of your family born, get married and die under his effigy because this has become part of our morals and customs. Behaving like those who went to see the lions devouring the first Christians, you also direct ironic smiles at those who believe in these writings, saying that they should spend some time in a psychiatric asylum. Nowadays, when someone has disturbing ideas, he or she is no longer crucified, or fed to wild animals – this is far too barbaric. Rather, such people are sent to a psychiatric asylum. Had these establishments existed two thousand years ago, Jesus and those who believed in him would have been confined there. As for those who believe in eternal life, ask them why they weep when they lose a loved one.

For as long as humankind was unable to understand the work of the Elohim scientifically, it was natural for people to believe in an impalpable 'God'. But now that, thanks to science, you understand that matter is infinitely large and infinitely small, you no longer have an excuse to believe in the 'God' that your primitive ancestors believed in. The Elohim, our creators, intend to be recognised by those who are capable now of understanding how life can be created, and can make the appropriate comparisons with ancient writings. Those people will have the right to eternity.

Christians! You have read a hundred times that Jesus would return – yet if he came back you would put him in a psychiatric asylum. Come, open your eyes.

Sons of Israel! You are still waiting for your Messiah – and yet you do not open the door.

Buddhists! Your writings indicate that the new Buddha will be born in the West. Recognise the anticipated signs.

Muslims! Mohammed reminded you that the Jewish people had made an error in killing the prophets, and that the Christians had also made an error in adoring their prophet more than the one who sent him. So welcome the last of the prophets, and love those who sent him.

If you recognise the Elohim as your creators, and if you love them and wish to welcome them, if you try to do good to other people by making as much use as you can of all your potential, if you think of your creators regularly, trying through telepathy to make them understand that you love them, if you help the Guide of Guides to accomplish his mission, you will without a doubt be entitled to scientific reincarnation on the planet of the eternals.

When humanity discovered the necessary form of energy to travel to the moon, it also came to possess sufficient energy to destroy all life on Earth. *'The hour has drawn near, and the moon is rent asunder'* it says in the Koran, Sura 54, verse 1. Therefore, any day now, humanity can destroy itself. Only those who follow the last of the prophets will be saved from destruction.

Long ago, people did not believe Noah and they laughed at him when he made preparations for the destruction. But they did not have the last laugh. When the Elohim told the inhabitants of Sodom and Gomorrah to leave the city without looking back, some did not heed those warnings, and were destroyed. Now that we have reached the stage when humanity itself may destroy all life on Earth, only those who recognise the Elohim as their creators will be saved from destruction. You may still not believe any of this, but when the time comes you will think of these lines again, and it will be too late.

When the cataclysm takes place – and there is a good chance it will happen quite soon, given the way human beings are presently behaving – there will be two sorts of people: those who have not recognised their creators and have not followed the last of the prophets, and those who have opened their eyes and ears and recognised what was made known a long time ago.

The former will undergo the suffering and destruction in the final furnace, and the latter will be spared and taken with the Guide of Guides to the planet of the eternals. There they will enjoy a marvellous life of fulfilment and pleasure with the sages of ancient times. It is they who will be waited on by magnificent athletes with beautifully sculptured bodies who will bring them sophisticated food to savour in the company of men and women of unequalled beauty and charm who will be entirely compliant to their desires.

> Seated on couches wrought with gold and jewels,
> Reclining thereon facing each other,
> There will wait on them youths, who will not age,
> Carrying goblets and ewers and cups filled out of a flowing spring,
> No headache will they get therefrom, nor will they be intoxicated,
> And carrying such fruits as they choose,
> And flesh of birds as they may desire,
> And there will be fair maidens with wide,
> Lovely eyes,
> Like pearls, we preserved,
> As a reward for what they did.
> *The Koran, Sura 56, Verses 15–24*

You who believe in all that is written here, when the Guide of Guides summons you somewhere, drop everything, for it might be because he has received some information concerning the end. If you are near him at that moment, you will be saved and taken away with him, far from the suffering.

You who believe, do not pass judgement on the words or deeds of the Elohim. The created do not have the right to judge their creator. Respect our prophet, and do not pass judgement on his actions or his words, for we hear through his ears, we see through his eyes, and we speak through his mouth. If you lack respect for the prophet, you lack respect for those who sent him, your creators.

The messages which were given earlier by the Elohim and all those people who adhered fully to them over the centuries, were right. But the obscurantist systems that were built on these messages using those who had a feeling for them were wrong. The Church is in the process of disappearing, and it deserves to disappear.

As for the men and women of the Church, let those who have their eyes open join the last of the prophets and help him spread throughout the world the latest message that has been handed to him. He will welcome them with open arms, and they will be able to blossom and fulfil themselves completely, while remaining the messengers of those in whom they had always believed. But this time they will at last truly comprehend what the Elohim's task was when they created humanity and when they sent Jesus.

They will really be able to fulfil themselves, released from the constraints of the Church which is fossilised and encrusted with crimes and criminal inquisitions thousands of years old. They will be able to do what they must do – make use of the organs their creators gave them, for our creators do not like us failing to use the organs they gave us.

The men and women of the Church will be able to enjoy their five senses and unite physically forever, or for an instant of happiness with whomsoever they please, without feeling guilty. It is now that they should feel guilty – guilty of not using all that was given to them by their creators. But released from their old constraints, they will truly open people's minds instead of putting them to sleep!

There are now hardly any students left in Roman Catholic seminaries where priests are trained. But there are some unhappy people who feel they have a vocation to spread love around them and open people's minds. Fifty years ago there were some 50,000 seminarists undergoing training at any one time but now there are only 500. This means that there are at least 49,500 unhappy people who have in them the potential to radiate the truth and harmony placed in them by our creators, but who do not feel attracted to a church shrouded with crimes and darkness.

You who are among those 49,500 people feeling a need to radiate the truth and do something for your fellow people, you who want to remain faithful to your creators and to Jesus, who told you to love one another and to respect your creators, 'the Father who is in heaven', you who feel that this message is true, come with us and become Guides.

Come and devote yourselves to the Elohim in the tradition of Moses, Elijah and Jesus, and to the spreading of their messages while continuing to live a normal life, truly fulfilling yourselves and enjoying all the senses that your creators gave you.

You who are presently members of the Church, take off those clothes that are as sad as their colour, the colour of the crimes that have been committed under their façade. Come with us, and become guides for humanity on the path of universal peace and love.

Leave those churches that are nothing but monuments built by primitive people, temples where they could adore worthless things – pieces of wood and metal. The Elohim do not need temples in every city to feel loved. It is sufficient that human beings try to communicate with them telepathically, thereby rediscovering the original meaning of prayer, but also opening themselves to infinity and not shutting themselves away in obscure, mystical stone buildings.

Hypocrisy and mystification have lasted long enough. Using truthful messages as their basis, organisations were built and grew fat on them, living in misplaced luxury and using people's fear to achieve their own ends. Wars were even waged under the pretext of spreading these messages abroad. Shame!

The money of the poor has been used to build a financial power base. Shame!

Love for one's neighbour has been preached with weapons in hand. Shame!

Human equality has been preached while supporting dictatorships. Shame!

'God is with us!' was said to encourage people to launch themselves into fratricidal wars. Shame!

Many times has the following Gospel passage been quoted: *'And you will make no man call you father upon the Earth: for you have only one Father. He who is in Heaven'* Matthew 23: 9.

Yet in the Church they make sure they themselves are constantly called 'Father' and 'Monsignor' and 'My Lord'. Shame!

Other texts have been read again and again that say: *'Do not take along any gold, nor silver nor brass in your purses. Take no bag for your journey, nor even a spare pair of shoes, nor coat nor yet staves.* Matthew 10: 9–10. Yet they have been wallowing in the luxury of the Vatican. Shame!

The Pope, if he does not sell all the properties of the Vatican to help unfortunate people, will not be admitted among the righteous on the planet of the eternals. It is shameful to wallow in luxury acquired at the expense of poor people by using true messages and by exploiting the births, marriages and deaths of human beings.

If all this changes, and if those people who were a part of that monstrous organisation without understanding their mistake now leave it and regret their error, they will be forgiven and entitled to eternity. For the Elohim, our creators, love us, their children, and forgive all those who sincerely regret their errors.

The Church has no reason to exist any longer, for it was entrusted with spreading the message of Jesus in anticipation of the age of the Apocalypse, and this age has now come. Also the Church has used methods of disseminating information that are a shame to it. Although it has accomplished its mission, the Church will be reproached for all its crimes, and those who still wear its clothes covered with blood will be among the guilty.

Wake up slumberer that you are! This is no fabricated story. Re-read all the writings of the ancient prophets, inform yourself about the most recent scientific discoveries – especially in biology – and look at the sky.

The predicted signs are there. The UFOs – unidentified flying objects – which mankind has dubbed 'flying saucers', are appearing every day. *'There will be signs in the sky'* – that was written a long time ago.

Once you have informed yourself of these things, integrate them all in your mind, and wake up. Claude Raël exists, he is indeed alive, and he has not written what Moses, Ezekiel, Elijah, Jesus, Muhammed, Buddha and all the others wrote. He is not a biologist, but he is the last of the line of prophets, the prophet of the Apocalypse – that is, of the time when everything can be understood.

He is living among you right now; you are lucky enough to be one of his contemporaries, and you are able to receive his teaching. Wake up! Pull yourself together, and take to the road. Go and see him, and help him – he needs you. You will be one of the pioneers of the final religion, the religion of religions, and you will have your place, whatever may happen, among the righteous for eternity, savouring the delights of the planet of the eternals, in the company of wonderfully pleasant beings who are ready to fulfil all your desires.

The Guides

YOU will follow the Guide of Guides, for he is the ambassador of the Elohim, our creators, 'our Fathers who art in Heaven'. You will follow all the advice that is given in this book, because it is the advice of your creators, transmitted by Claude Raël, our ambassador, the last of the prophets, the shepherd of shepherds, and you will help him to build the religion of religions.

Jews, Christians, Muslims, Buddhists and all you who have other religions, open your eyes and your ears, re–read your holy writings, and you will understand that this book is the last one, the one predicted by your own prophets. Come and join us to prepare for the coming of our creators.

Write to the Guide of Guides, and he will put you in touch with other people who, like you, are Raëlians – that is, people who understand the message transmitted by Claude Raël. He will put you in touch with a guide in your region so that you may meet regularly to meditate, and act to spread this message, so that it becomes known throughout the world.

You who are reading this message, be aware that you are privileged, and think of all those who do not yet know about it. Do all you can to make sure that no one around you is ignorant of these fantastic revelations, without ever trying to convince those to whom you speak. Bring this message to their notice and if they are ready, they will open up by themselves. Constantly repeat to yourself this sentence of Gandhi's: 'It is not because no one sees the truth that it becomes an error'.

You who feel such joy in reading this message, and who wish to radiate this truth and make it shine around you, you who want to live by devoting yourself totally to our creators by applying scrupulously what they ask, by training to guide humanity on the path of blossoming and fulfilment, you should become a Guide if you want to be fully capable of this.

Write to the Guide of Guides, to Claude Raël, and he will make you welcome and arrange an initiation which will enable you to radiate this truth fully. For you can open the minds of others only if your own mind is open.

The love of the creators for their work is immense, and you should return this love to them. You must love them as they love you, and prove it by assisting their ambassador and his helpers, putting all your means and all your strength at their service so that they may travel all over the world to spread this message and build an embassy to welcome our creators.

If you wish to help me realise the goals set by the Elohim, write to me, Claude Raël at: The International Raëlian Movement, Case Postale 225, CH 1211 Geneva 8, Switzerland.

Also do not forget that regular local meetings of people who believe in this final message are held on the first Sunday of April, on 6 August, 7 October and 13 December each year. The venues for these meetings will be set out in the liaison bulletin of the Raëlian Movement of your country and some addresses to help you make contact are listed at the end of this book.

AUTHOR'S POSTSCRIPT – 1997

MANY things have happened since I wrote the two books that now make up this first edition to be published commercially in Britain, the British Commonwealth and the United States. I originally published *The Book Which Tells the Truth* privately in my own language in France in 1974 and followed it with *Extra-Terrestrials Took Me To Their Planet* in 1976.

Until now I have added nothing whatsoever to those two original texts. Meantime they have been translated into twenty-five languages by volunteer Raëlian supporters and more than a million copies of my books have been sold worldwide. Until now all previous English versions of the books have been printed, published and distributed under the control of the International Raëlian Movement, first from Canada, then later from Japan.

This specially re-translated volume is the first fully commercial publication of my writings anywhere in the world and I am confident this will bring the understandings they contain to an ever wider audience.

During these first twenty-four years of its existence, the International Raëlian Movement has grown steadily and at present has a total of about 40,000 active members worldwide. National branches of the IRM are now established in eighty-four countries, including all the world's major nations, and people are coming forward all the time to help make this extraordinary final message of the Elohim better known.

More good people are still needed, but at the time of writing, the Movement is strongest in France, Canada and Japan. It is also expanding strongly in the United States, Australia, South East Asia, Latin America and Africa, as well as in Britain and most of the other countries of Europe. More recently new national branches of the Movement have been founded in Hawaii, China and South Africa.

During the late 1970s and early 1980s I wrote and published further books which served to amplify the information in this volume. In their

English versions they were entitled *Let's Welcome Our Fathers From Space* (1979) and *Sensual Meditation* (1980).

At regular seminars held in every continent of the world since then, the teachings of the Elohim which I have set down in these books have been passed on to many thousands of people of all ages by myself and senior members of the IRM. In all there are now around 130 guides, or Raëlian priests, worldwide.

The Movement also publishes an international quarterly glossy magazine, *Apocalypse*, in which I and other leading Raëlians write of current developments. This publication helps to disseminate further the philosophies and insights of the Elohim.

Preparations to build the secure embassy requested by the Elohim are also progressing well. The embassy and residence need to be protected by extra-territorial rights like any normal international diplomatic mission and in accordance with the Elohim's precise instructions, Raëlian architects have already completed commissioned drawings for the complex of buildings where the most dramatic and extraordinary meeting of world government leaders in history will take place. Not long after we built a small scale model of the embassy based on these drawings, a crop circle appeared in England which bore an astonishing resemblance to it. Around seven million dollars have been raised so far towards building the embassy and money continues to be donated.

But I have to say that finance is not the chief obstacle to the completion of this project. The political and diplomatic problems are a thornier issue and to overcome them patience and perseverance will be required.

In this regard, the International Raëlian Movement has several times since 1991 made representations to the Israeli Government and to the Chief Rabbi in Jerusalem, requesting that the necessary extra-territoriality be granted so that the embassy may be built close to Jerusalem where the Elohim created the first human beings. The first temple of the Jewish religion was in fact a previous embassy around which the ancient city was built. The Elohim are now waiting for the State of Israel to grant such extra-territorial status for the new embassy – the third temple – but so far there has been no positive response from Israel.

The first approach was made on 8 November 1991 at the Jewish New Year and another official request was made to Israel's Chief Rabbi some months later. The request was acknowledged and a study of the application was begun. In the summer of 1993 an Israeli government commission concluded that the Raëlian Movement was peaceful in intent and was of no threat to Israel's security. In their report, two rabbis concluded that it would be 'better not to do anything against Raël in case he really is the awaited Messiah'.

In November 1993 a further direct request was made to Israel's prime minister, Yitzhak Rabin, when he was in Canada attending the Montreal Jewish Convention. But after a month Mr. Rabin replied through one of his office representatives that he could not grant it.

If Israel ultimately declines to allow a grant of extra-territoriality, as already indicated, we will most likely establish the embassy on Palestinian or Egyptian territory or in another neighbouring state. In fact the lower slopes of Mount Sinai would make an excellent alternative choice, since that is where Yahweh, the leader of the Elohim, first appeared to Moses.

Nevertheless the Elohim would prefer to give Israel the opportunity to agree to this request since that is the whole purpose of the State of Israel. Already in 1990, as a sign of their special feelings towards the people of Israel, they agreed to my suggestion to modify their original Symbol of Infinity when used by Raëlian Movements in the West. The central swastika, which means 'well-being' in Sanskrit and also represents infinity in time, was replaced with a galaxy-shaped swirl. This change was made in an effort to help the negotiations for building the embassy of the Elohim in Israel and also out of respect for the sensitivities of the victims who suffered and died under the Nazi swastika during the Second World War. In Asia, where the swastika can be found in most Buddhist temples and where it represents infinity in time, the original symbol is not a problem.

This modification of the IRM symbol for the West was, of course, gladly made and when looking back now and surveying our progress since 1973, I can see that everything is going according to plan. The International Raëlian Movement will one day achieve all the goals set by the Elohim – with or without my participation. I know it has become self sustaining and could now function perfectly well without me.

A lot still remains to be done and even when at last the great day dawns and the Elohim land openly and officially before the eyes of world government leaders and an international array of television cameras and media representatives, some sceptics, I expect, will still continue to doubt whether these highly advanced human beings could truly have created all life artificially on our planet. The leading members of the IRM and myself are aware this might be so. But this does not daunt us – quite the reverse.

Since 1973 scientific research has continued to confirm the essence of the information given to me then by the Elohim. Most notably this year in Britain, it was announced that Scottish scientists had succeeded in cloning a sheep. This landmark event in human scientific history made it clear that very soon the cloning of human beings will be possible. Just as on the Elohim's planet it will become a means for human beings to achieve 'eternal' life. No ethics committee in the world will be able to prevent human beings from wishing to do this.

The next steps required will be those that make possible the transfer of mental information, memory and personality from an aging individual into a new, physically young adult clone. This transfer of memory directly into a young adult means that effectively the same individual can live indefinitely. Human laws will have to be adapted to our changing culture and increasing technological advances and I am very proud to have created Clonaid, the first human cloning company which can now be contacted on the Internet at its website 'clonaid.com.' These are still early days for all such issues but new laws will have to be passed to define criteria setting out who will be allowed to benefit from these technologies. Here, as on the Elohim's planet, the number of clones will also need to be limited to one per individual – and then only after death.

The Elohim themselves will land here on Earth in the not too distant future. It will be no longer than thirty-eight years and might be much sooner – if the truth I have described in this book spreads more rapidly around the world. The Elohim will bring with them all the great prophets of the past, including Moses, Elijah, the Buddha, Jesus Christ and Mohammed.

This long-awaited event will be the most wonderful day in the history of humanity. I hope you will be present when they land at their embassy and are able to share the joy of knowing that you were part of this wonderful adventure and that you helped financially to build it.

The area where the embassy is to be built will become the spiritual centre of the world in the next millennium. People from all nations will come in pilgrimage to this holy place. A replica of the embassy will be built near the real one and opened to the public so that they can see what it is like inside.

But will the Raëlian Movement's mission end with the coming of our creators? Not at all. On the contrary, it will be the real *beginning* of our mission. With the disappearance of all primitive religions, the vacuum will have to be filled with a new spirituality – one that is in tune with the technological revolution still to come.

We are now today's human beings using tomorrow's technology, with yesterday's religions and yesterday's thinking. Thanks to the Elohim, we will be able to reach new spiritual levels by embracing their own religion – an atheist one – that of infinity as represented by their symbol. The Guides of the Raëlian Movement will become the priests of this new religion, allowing human beings to feel in harmony with the infinitely small and the infinitely great, allowing them to realise we are stardust and energies for ever.

Laboratories and universities will be built close to the embassy and there, under the guidance of the Elohim, human scientists will be able to improve their knowledge. In this way we will gradually approach the Elohim's scientific level. This will enable us to venture out to other planets to create life ourselves and we will become in our own turn 'Elohim' for those we create.

Spirituality and science will work together free at last from the medieval fears that have haunted our past. This will enable us to become 'gods' ourselves as was written long ago in the ancient scriptures.

But let's first build the embassy!

Raël,
Quebec
Canada
Summer 1997

APPENDIX

A New Message from the Elohim, December 13, 1997

Shortly after the initial printing of this English edition of The Final Message but before publication and this first re-print, a new message was received from the Elohim. The text is as follows:

It is now twenty-four years since we gave our final Message to men and women of the Earth through the mouth of our beloved son and prophet Rael - the one which, as predicted, came to destroy the 'mystery of God'. It is twenty-four years too, that you Raelians, who have officially and publicly recognised us as your creators, have been working so that we may be welcomed in the embassy we requested. Your devotion and your efforts have warmed our hearts and the most faithful of you will be among those rewarded.

In all religions there are people who deserve our love but Raelians are the closest to us. They are our new chosen people and one day will have their new promised land - because their love is based on consciousness and understanding and not on blind faith.

Those who loved us thinking we were one or several supernatural gods were precious in our eyes - and in pre-scientific times, they had no choice anyway. But those who continue to love us and even love us more while knowing that we are made in their image and not supernatural, those people touch us much more deeply and will be rewarded even more because they love us with their consciousness and not just with their faith. For it is consciousness which makes them similar to us.

We had asked that an Embassy be built to welcome us near Jerusalem, and the authorities of the stiff-necked people have refused several times to give their authorisation and grant the status of extra-territoriality. Our preference for Jerusalem was purely sentimental, because for us Jerusalem is everywhere where people love us, respect us and wish to welcome us with due respect. The chosen people are those who knowing who we are, wish to welcome us - and those people are the Raelians. The true Jews on Earth are no longer the people of Israel but those who recognise us as their creators and wish to see us return.

The link we have with the people of Isreal is about to be broken and the new Covenant is coming to an end. They have very little time to understand their mistake before being dispersed once again.

Meanwhile we must now address to all nations on Earth our request for the status of extra-territoriality that is needed to establish our embassy; and the one kilometre radius that is required can just as well consist of water as of dry land - on the condition that navigation be prohibited within that radius.

As soon as another country gives this authorisation, Israel will be offered a last chance to grant its own authorisation during a very limited period of reflection. If they do not, the Embassy will be built elsewhere and the people of David will lose our protection and be dispersed.

The country which will grant the necessary extra-territorial status and see the Embassy built on its territory - or on territory it gives or sells - will have a guaranteed and flourishing future. It will benefit from our protection and will become the spiritual and scientific centre of the whole planet for the millenniums to come.

The hour of our Great Return is near and we will support and protect the most devoted ones among you. Your enemies will increasingly see our all-powerful arm strike them, particularly the usurper of Rome, his bishops and all those who act in our name without our mandate.

The year 2,000 is nothing for us and nothing for a very large majority of people on Earth who are not Christians. But many false prophets will try to use this change of millennium to mislead human beings. This has been foreseen and is, in fact, a means of selecting the most conscious. Follow your Guide of Guides, he will know how to avoid the dangers of this time of transition because he is the Way, the Truth and the Life.

Buddhism is more and more successful on Earth and this is good as it is the religion closest to the Truth and to the new scientific-spiritual balance necessary for human beings of the new age. Buddhism, stripped of its mystical past is Raelism and more and more Buddhists will become Raelians.

May your joy in seeing our Great Return approach, give you wings to overcome the last obstacles of the journey. We are so close to this day and to you that whenever you meditate and collect yourselves, you should be able to feel our presence...

And this feeling will illuminate your days and nights and will make your life wonderful no matter what difficulties remain to be overcome. The pleasure of meeting us will be much less than the pleasure of having worked for this day to arrive. It is in the act of accomplishing your mission that the greater pleasure lies, not in its result.

In the meantime, from the mouth of our Beloved Prophet, our Love and our light will guide you: and don't forget that even if we do see you permanently, each time he looks at you we see you to even greater advantage because he beautifies what he sees with the love he has for you...

The more you love him, the more you love us because he is a part of us on Earth. If you find it difficult sometimes to show us your affection it is because you do not have the consciousness to realise that our Beloved Son is again treading the same ground as you in a new time.

You cannot love us and at the same time neglect him, because once again, nobody comes to the Father but through the Son. Because he *is* amongst you, eating when you eat, sleeping when you sleep, laughing when you laugh and crying when you cry. You cannot claim to love us if you do not treat him as the dearest one of all among us.

His love for you is so great that he constantly asks us to forgive things we find unforgivable. He is your best advocate in the eyes of your Creators. Also, on your planet where Love and Forgiveness are increasingly rare in a society which is becoming more and more barbaric because of a lack of these values, he is your most precious gift.

You lack love? Look at him, he is alive and living amongst you!

May his light guide you to us whether we return or not because in either case we await you among our eternals.

Peace and love to all Human Beings of goodwill.

FURTHER INFORMATION
FROM THE AUTHOR

RÈADERS may wish to contact the author or his organisation, the International Raëlian Movement (IRM) for further information about this book and other related matters. The main global address for the author is: **c/o The International Raëlian Movement, Case Postale 225, CH-1211, Geneva 8, Switzerland.**

A number of other contact addresses related to different areas of the world are given below. Readers should address queries and requests to the address most appropriate for them. The Tagman Press is not responsible for conveying any information or delivering any materials that may be offered.

North and South America
Canadian Raëlian Movement, PO Box 86, Youville Station,
Montreal, Quebec, Canada H2P 2V2. Phone: 1514 681 6263
United States Raëlian Movement. PO Box 611793. North Miami, FL
33261 USA . Phone: 305 273 0553

Africa
Mouvement Raëlien Africain, O5 BP 1444, Abidjan O5, Cote d'Ivoire

Asia
Japanese Raëlian Movement, Sagawa Building 2-A, Kita-Otsuka 2-6-8
Tokyo-To, Toshima Ku, Japan. Fax: 813 3916 7221. Phone: 813 3916 7080

Europe, the Middle East and the Indian Sub-continent
International Raëlian Movement, Case Postale 225, CH 1211, Geneva 8,
Switzerland

United Kingdom
British Raëlian Movement, BCM Minstrel, London WC1N 3XX. Phone: 0181 659 7676
Australia
Australian Raëlian Movement, PO Box 2397, Sydney, New South Wales 2001, Australia

Internet addresses:
Raelian Movement Homepage www. rael. org
Clonaid Homepage www. clonaid. com
Ufoland Homepage www. ufoland. com

ACKNOWLEDGEMENTS

THANKS are due to the Phototeque Archive of the International Raelian Movement (IRM) in Le Mans for permission to use the photographs on pages 105 to 108 in which the IRM holds the copyright.

Similar thanks are due to George Wingfield for permission to use the crop circle aerial photograph which he took at Cheesefoot Head in Wiltshire, England in August 1990.

A number of individuals generously gave time, energy and their talents in assisting with the translation, design and production of this edition including Angela Hind in London and Marcus Wenner in Tokyo as well as Guner Behic in Florida, Michael Claibourne in Los Angeles, and Brigid Chapman and Mike Bennett in the United Kingdom.

For the translations of the many Biblical quotations in the book, the texts of the New English Bible, the King James Bible and the New International Bible have been used as references.

Cover design: Jim Wilkie

Other books by Raël to be published by the Tagman Press

SENSUAL MEDITATION

An important companion volume to *The Final Message*.

To open our minds to the future and realise our true potential we must learn to awaken our bodies more fully to the pleasures of all our senses . . . that is the vital lesson which Raël claims to have brought back from his journey to another planet. In this volume he details the techniques of meditation which he says the Elohim have designed to help bring us into harmony with the infinite nature of all things. By helping us to enjoy sounds, colours, tastes, perfumes and caresses more intensely, he says, the teachings enable us to find new creativity within ourselves. Like *The Final Message* this book combines new re-translations of two privately published English-language volumes. They are: *Let's Welcome Our Fathers from Space* and *Sensual Meditation*. It also provides answers to the questions most frequently asked about the controversial contents of *The Final Message* and contains further revelations which Raël says the Elohim instructed him to withhold from his first two books.

GENIOCRACY

The first English translation of a highly controversial political thesis.

Democracy is an imperfect form of government destined to give way to rule by geniuses – 'geniocracy'. Under this system, no candidate for high office may stand for election unless his or her intelligence level is measurably fifty per cent above the norm. Furthermore, to be eligible to vote, an elector must have an intelligence level ten per cent above the average. Geniocracy is therefore selective democracy. These challenging concepts, according to Raël, already apply on the planet of the Elohim. Unless we can come up with something better, he says, they advise us to begin preparing to implement a similar system, since all human progress is ultimately dependent on the work of geniuses.

In this first edition of the book to be published in the English language, Raël describes how such a process might work here – once intelligence testing is sufficiently developed.